Bernard Gotlieb

"Hey, What Happened To You?"

The story of the longest survivor of a bone marrow transplant for leukemia in Canada.

The Procedure has become more simplified and efficient today, thanks to medical research and the generosity of donors.

I dedicate this book to my mother, Ray Gotlieb.
I would like to thank:

-Dr. Stephen Caplan, hematologist at the Jewish General Hospital in Montreal;

-Dr. Hans Messner, hematologist at the Princess Margaret Hospital in Toronto;

-Dr. Robin Billick, dermatologist at the Jewish General Hospital in Montreal;

-my sister Gloria who so generously donated her bone marrow to me;

-other members of my family and all those who donated their blood;

-Mrs. Valérie Legault-Heria who authorized the use of the Héma-Québec's text;

-Claire Brouillet, who helped me write my story

-My father, Manny Gotlieb, who was after me from day one of the transplant to write about my experience.

Hey! What Happened to You?

Upon seeing me on a stretcher in the airplane, an American passenger asked me, without caring at all for my response, "Hey, what happened to you?"
It was 1979. I was 21 years old. I was coming home after a 3-month stay at the Princess Margaret Hospital in Toronto. I had just undergone one of the first bone marrow transplants for treating leukemia in Canada. It was still in an experimental stage.
What happened to me…?
I am 53 today and I am reliving, in all serenity, the film of events that have turned my life upside down.

Foreword

Since 1979, the year I underwent a bone marrow transplant for leukemia, I overcame multiple complications as a result of this procedure which hadn't yet been perfected.

Along my journey, I came across refined people: researchers, doctors, nurses, relatives and friends thanks to whom I was able to overcome stoically, I could even say serenely, different struggles that life presented.

My father was always after me to write my life story: he said it could interest people and help them.

As I was hoping in all impartiality that this bone marrow transplant marked an important step in Canadian medical research, I had kept my notes and those of my mother. Thus I was able to find dates of different medical procedures I underwent and the names of doctors and different specialists… All these people helped take care of me as much with their heart as with their hands. Alas, I am not a writer, I had on hand all the pertinent documents, but I didn't know how to go about it.

As luck would have it, I was put in touch with someone who helped me write my story: she persisted that I put my ideas in order to finally relate this story which was to be filled with difficult periods, not to mention often comical ones as well.

A HAPPY CHILD: AN ADOLESCENT... THREATENED

-A boy like any other
I grew up in Cote St. Luc, a middle-class community. I knew all the neighbours on my street. I had a lot of friends my age with whom I used to play.
I went to Westminster Elementary School for the first 3 grades of school and then to the new Wentworth School, which had just opened at the time of Canada's centennial in 1967. I made some good friends there.

-Spoiled by all
Really, I had a very happy childhood: I was always spoiled by my mother. When I had a pain, be it physical or emotional, it was she who really felt it.
My dear mother anticipated my desires and would help me with my homework. She used to give me money to buy a challah (a Jewish bread) for the Sabbath at the corner store. This included $1.00 to buy myself 7 chocolate bars, allowing me to keep the change.
As for my 2 older sisters, they used to take me in their arms and drive me crazy with love. They made me sing and dance. They even taught me Chubby Checkers' "The Twist" so well that, at the age of 4, I was on The Magic Tom television show.
I had practiced it so many times before going on air, that by the time Magic Tom asked me to dance before him, I was unable to give my usual performance because I was so exhausted!

I learnt to play the game better from my Uncle Jack, the game that I would later make my life passion.

-Liking team sports
I was not very good at sports, but a few I really liked, like ball hockey and wiffleball. We used to play in the street, my friends and I: it was I who organized the games for the guys. I was also a fan of bowling but, there too, I wasn't very good.

Nonetheless, it was fun to be part of the team who bowled every week. I used to keep score.

-Crazy about Scrabble® (1)
Even as a youngster, I was fascinated by the game of Scrabble®. The family champ was my Uncle Jack, a lawyer. It was a real challenge to play against him. I suspect I really learned to play the game well from my uncle, this game that I would later make my life passion.

-Fearing only one thing: the sight of blood
The sight of blood always made me weak. If I injured myself, I was unable to look at the blood.

I remember one day at school, we were watching a documentary film on road accidents.
Even if I knew they were only actors using fake blood, I had to leave the classroom as I was feeling faint.

Well, in my case, blood plays a very important role as the story unfolds.

---

(1) Scrabble® is a registered trademark. All rights reserved in the United States and Canada by Hasbro Inc., and in the rest of the world, J.W. Spear & Sons Ltd., an affiliate of Mattel Inc.

Even though I knew well that they were actors and it was fake blood.

-A routine test triggers the alarm!
During the winter of 1977 when I was 19, I went to Florida with my mother by plane. Upon returning and for a few days following, my ears were a little blocked. I consulted with a G.P., Dr. Michael Gold, a doctor who I met at a summer camp and who had just opened a practice near me.

This doctor requested for all new patients a blood test, a chest X-ray and cardiogram.

A few days later I got a call from Dr. Gold asking me to come back to his office to redo the blood test that he had me take at the Montreal General Hospital. I returned to see him, even though I wasn't keen on blood tests!

-A problem with my blood?
Not long afterwards, Dr. Gold called me back to tell me he had detected some irregularities in my blood. He referred me to Dr. Stephen Caplan, a hematologist at the Jewish General Hospital with whom he had already made an appointment for me.

-My father's worry
My father, more concerned than I, accompanied me to Dr. Caplan who took a bone marrow biopsy.

At the doctor's request, we waited there for the result of the analysis. The longer the wait, the more my dad was getting nervous. As for me, I was in a dream.

Finally, Dr. Caplan invited us into his office. Alas, the analysis confirmed his concerns. I was a carrier of the "Philadelphia chromosone" which meant that I had leukemia!

- I have leukemia!
Here I am stricken with a deadly disease at such a young age!

-Dr. Caplan takes the time to talk to us
He explained to us that leukemia is a cancer of blood cells: among people who have the disease, the bone marrow is the seat of production of abnormally elevated white cells (they protect the body against infections and viruses and can multiply their number in case of attack).

These leukemic cells, in multiplying themselves in the bone marrow in an inordinate way, end up overwhelming the platelets and healthy red cells. In my case, the analysis showed I had around 16,000 white cells (leukocytes) per cubic millimeter of blood, while healthy adults have normally between 5,000 to 10,000.

The leukemia I was suffering from was chronic myelogenous leukemia (CML), a kind of leukemia normally found among people 50 years or older... It was as intriguing as it was worrisome.

The doctor was of the opinion however, that since I was only 19 and otherwise seemed in good shape, this leukemia would only slowly develop. He said to me, "You are in good health: take advantage of it and live well! We won't intervene for the time being, but we will analyze your blood every month". Had I never taken that initial blood test, I would have never known that I had leukemia: I felt perfectly fine.

-My father is upset
The news of my disease shocked my father. He, who I always knew to be so strong, was more shaken than I. I heard him speak with the doctor.

It was as if they were speaking about someone else.

My dad asked the doctor for explanations as to the possible cause of this disease, something unique to the family.

The doctor inquired about my past experiences, but we saw nothing in particular up until then.

Nevertheless, when the doctor asked me if I had ever been exposed to toxic products like benzene…I remember that among the manual labour jobs I had done the previous spring, I had used a very strong cleaning agent while doing some handy work. Were these toxic fumes the cause of my problem? He couldn't say for sure.

-Stunned, I return to my classes
As for me, since I felt in top physical form, I saw no reason to change my daily program.

I kissed my father and left the doctor's office. I returned to my course at l'Université de Montréal in Hispanic studies.

On that day, I must admit, I was a student rather distracted…It was bizarre: I felt like an intruder in the classroom. Was there still a place for me among these healthy young people?

-The whole family in caucus…
When I came home that night, I saw the whole family was gathered in my parents' room. I must say that I am the youngest of 4 children: my older brother is Fred and my 2 sisters are Sharon and Gloria. They were all there to worry about me. Only my mother wasn't there: she was very busy organizing an evening with the women neighbours. I went straight to my room that is next to my parents'. Evidently, they were talking about me.
I heard sobs and murmurs as if I had received the death sentence!
I felt they were crying for me. I was really overwhelmed. Moved. Powerless.

-And everyone is going to get involved
From that moment on, all family members began to familiarize themselves with the disease that was attacking me.
My dad had bought some books on medicine where I read that it was possible that my system lacked iron. So I forced myself to eat liver, me who hated liver. Needless to say, that was not a miracle remedy!

-For me, attested armour: stoicism
I was familiar with blood, this red liquid that comes out of wounds and whose mere sight made me feel weak.

I wanted to study this fluid a bit closer.

I began to understand the battle that was going on inside my body. I found it interesting but I didn't indulge in self-pity. I faced the facts in a stoic way, as if it concerned someone else. I took things as they came: I just dealt with them.

-I know I am not alone.
I received a lot of support from my family which was and still remains my comfort: my aunts, my uncles and my cousins, everyone worried about me.
I believe my family was never so united than at that difficult period.

I was, indeed, very much alive and I felt in very good shape.

THE COMPONENTS OF BLOOD

Plasma

Plasma constitutes 55% of the total volume of blood. Made up of 90% water, salt, lipids and hormones, plasma is above all a liquid rich in proteins, which includes albumin (its principle protein), immunoglobulins as well as coagulation and fibrinogen.

Plasma fulfills several functions: transporting of blood cells and nutritive substances; regulation of water and of the organism's mineral salts; irrigation of tissues; defense against infections and blood coagulation.

The albumin contained in the plasma prevents the blood from losing too much water and thickening when it circulates through the permeable, narrow water vessels (capillaries). Albumin transports diverse blood components and nutritive substances. Moreover, immunoglobulins in the plasma are the antibodies which play an important role with the white blood cells in the defense against pathogenic agents. Then, coagulation factors are responsible along with the platelets in stopping hemorrhages.

A deficit can bring about an inability to retain water in the vessels (albumin), a reduction of the organism's immune defenses (immunoglobulins), or abnormalities of the blood's coagulation (factors of coagulation).

Red blood cells

White blood cells and platelets are found suspended in the plasma. A drop of blood the size of a pinhead contains around 5 million red blood cells, or red blood corpuscles. They are little biconcave discs without a nucleus and whose red colour is due to a protein called hemoglobin, a protein containing iron. Among women, the mass of red blood cells occupies from 37 to 43% of the volume of blood; among men, from 43 to 49%. The red blood cell's function is to transport oxygen.

White Blood Cells
A little larger than red blood cells, they fulfill diverse functions of purification and protection against infections. In effect, the moment an infection is present somewhere in the human body, the white cells go there to fight it off.

Platelets
Platelets (or thrombocytes) are minute blood cells. Their function is to contribute to blood coagulation and wound healing.
fondation@hema-quebec,qc.ca

AN UNEXPECTED GIFT: A TRIP TO ISRAEL!

One month after the doctor's verdict, my parents – who feared for me and who, without a doubt feared the worst – decided to offer me the best gift a young Jew could wish for – a trip to Israel!
My parents wanted to take advantage of an opportunity that was coming up: a Jewish association, the Hillel group, was organizing a 6-week trip to Israel for Jewish adolescents.

Obviously, they must have said to themselves, "While he's still alive…"

I was indeed very much alive and I felt in very good shape. I was going to very much enjoy such a marvelous trip. The doctor allowed me to go on the condition that I take a blood test there every 3 weeks and send him the results. It was perfect! I was 20 years old. I didn't even have the time to hope to go to Israel one day!

-This trip is a great gift of a lifetime
I left with a very enthusiastic bunch of characters. Some people were very colourful! I quickly became friends with Earl Teitelbaum from Chomedey, Laval, a student in medicine at McGill University, and who today is a cardiologist in Toronto.

ARRIVING IN ISRAEL!

Before landing in Israel, what a surprise it was for us to hear the Israeli national anthem being played on the plane.

It was very moving. I felt proud of my roots.

THE NATIONAL ANTHEM OF ISRAEL

כל עוד בלבב פנימה נפש יהוד י הומיה,

ולפאתי מזרח קדימה עין לציון צופיה,

עוד לא אבדה תקותנו התקוה בת שנות אלפים,

להיות עם חופשי בארצנו,

אֹרֶץ ציון וירושלים.

להיות עם חופשי בארצנו,

ארץ ציון וירושלים.

> In the Jewish heart
> A Jewish spirit still sings
> And the eyes look east toward Zion
> Our hope is not lost,
> Our hope of two thousand years,
> To be a free nation in our land
> In the land of Zion and Jerusalem

The Ben Gurion Airport in Tel-Aviv was packed and exciting.
I realized I was really in a small country of big importance.
It was very different from North America which I had never left until then.

-Truly, I was far from home!
Outside, it was hot. The countryside was brown, as if burnt by the sun. Everywhere there were signs in Hebrew, English and Arabic. Everyone was running. There was a bustle I wasn't quite used to.

Kibbutz Ramot Menashe

KIBBUTZ RAMOT MENASHE

-My first experience in Israel: the kibbutz
For 3 ½ weeks, we worked on Kibbutz Ramot Menash in the north of Israel, 30 km. from Haifa.

Upon arrival, they assigned us little cabins which 2 people shared.

We got up around 5:30 a.m. to do the big work before sunrise.

The group was divided into groups that were responsible for different tasks. Me, I first picked oranges, and then worked in the kitchen helping to prepare meals.

We always ate in a large dining hall for the entire kibbutz, about 200 people.

The lunch meal, a buffet, was the most diversified and abundant: we had all afternoon to burn off the ingested calories.

-A warm experience
When we left the kibbutz, we felt closer together after this life experience on a commune where everyone did their part in a friendly way.

We were ready to embark on the big trip together.

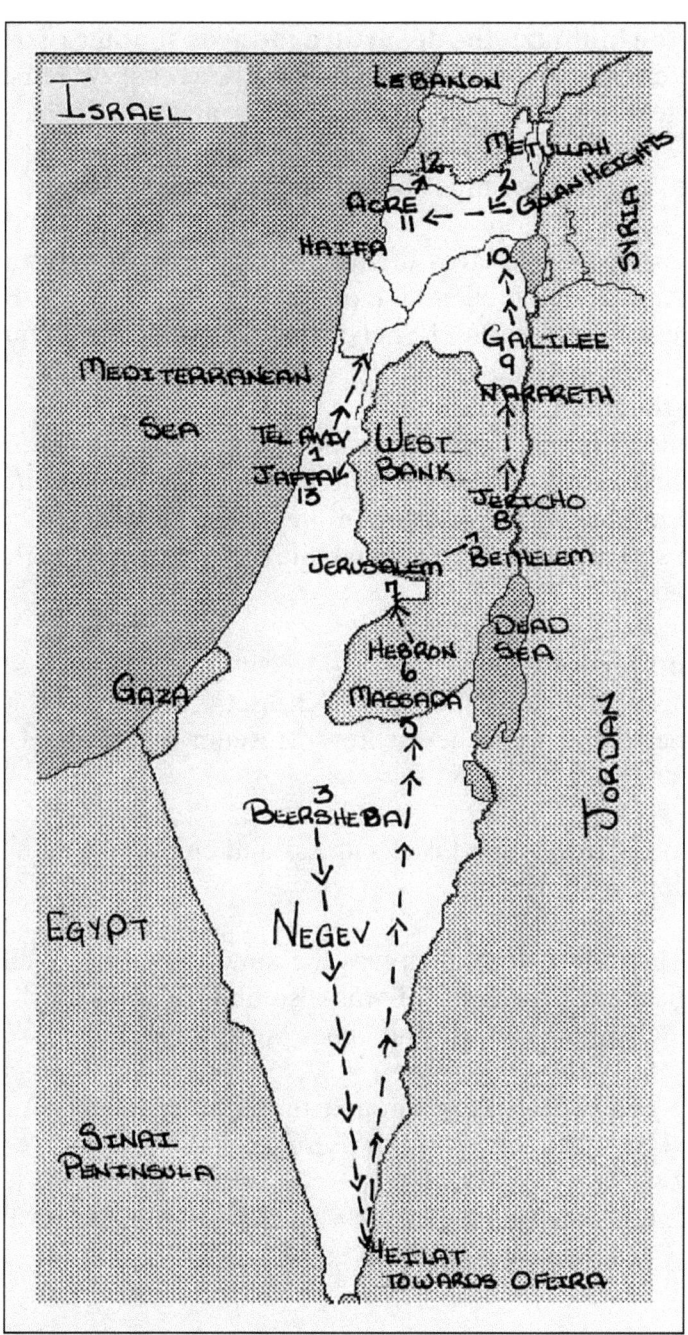

-After the kibbutz: the departure towards southern Israel!
We were going to visit the country for 2 ½ weeks! We first headed completely south, passing by Jerusalem and Beersheba, right to Sharm-el-Sheik, the southernmost point of the Sinai Desert that Israel still held at the time and which they called Ofira.

It was fascinating to cross the Negev and Sinai Deserts and to see Saudi Arabia on the other side of the Red Sea. We saw Bedouins in the desert. At Sharm-el-Sheik, we did some scuba diving.

-From the Sinai, northbound
We visited Masada where the zealots, those extreme patriots, lived in the first century A.D. By the hundreds, they committed mass suicide in their fortress on top of the mountain to avoid becoming Roman slaves. As for us, as good tourists, we then went floating in the Dead Sea.

-Visiting Jerusalem
In Jerusalem we visited the Knesset, which is the Israeli Parliament, and then the Hebrew Museum where the Dead Sea scrolls are held.

We also visited, with a lot of sadness and emotion, Yad Vashem – the Holocaust Museum.

The high point of Jerusalem was the famous Wailing Wall, one of the holiest sites for Jews. I was also able to walk on the temple mount, where the el-Aqsa and Omar Mosques are found.

I really enjoyed walking through the Arab markets. As a good tourist, I bought a few souvenir presents.

Jerusalem is a fascinating city. It's a city full of history. There are so many fabulous sites to discover.

It is also a city full of contrasts: one finds the ancient and modern side by side, the religious and the secular, Jewish people and Arab people, the bustling city and the Judean Desert right next to it. It's obviously this city that touched me the most.

-A certain worrisome environment
As a visiting Jew, I did not suffer the stress that Israeli citizens felt living with the Arabs. It was not peace but what you would call a troubling state of non-war…

You'd see the soldiers walking around everyone with sub-machine guns. I was not that concerned as I felt secure.

The citizens themselves tried to live the most normally possible, like families going to the beach, going shopping and doing their daily activities.

-Continuing northbound
Continuing our trip towards Israel's north, we arrived at the pretty city of Haifa. We visited the famous Bahai Temple with its golden roof.

We went right up to the Lebanese border to Metullah, a place called "The Good Fence". We also passed by coastal cities like Acre and Caesarea before arriving in Jaffa, one of the oldest cities in the world.

It was the end of our tour in Israel.

One cannot help but notice while crossing the country, what the Israelis have done. They transformed the desert into habitable land, they made it bloom and produce fruit trees and each piece of land is used to the fullest.

-The group farewells
Once the tour was over, it wasn't without emotion that we said good-bye to each other after such a remarkable experience.

Some people among us were going to stay longer in Israel; others would take the plane back to Canada and the lucky ones were going to do a stopover in a European country before returning to Canada.

-Thanks to cousins, I can prolong my stay!
As for me, I had an opportunity to prolong my stay in Israel before returning by plane: I stayed 15 days at some cousins, first in Jerusalem and then in Tel-Aviv with other cousins!

I was therefore able to get an insight into daily life there. In so doing, we walked in the city and its surroundings, we went to the beach and we ate in the house and in restaurants.

I tried to take in this entire atmosphere.

-Medically…
Even though I didn't at all feel the need, I fulfilled Dr. Caplan's conditions: I went to have my blood checked twice at a Chupat Cholim, a medical clinic.

The white cell count hovered around 25,000/mm^3, which was acceptable.

-In addition to Israel, a nice stopover in Spain!
My experience did not end with Israel. I was on my way to Spain for 3 weeks with Earl Teitelbaum. En route to Spain, we had a 3-hour stopover to change planes in Rome. We hired a cab and ran to see the Roman Forum and Coliseum – it was an opportunity!

I was the one who suggested Spain. As I had taken a beginner's course in Spanish at the Cegep level and others at university, I believed I would find myself in familiar territory! Evidently, I was soon going to learn that it takes a lot more to be able to manage with real Spaniards!

We were able to visit, albeit summarily, the big cities of southern Spain.

-First of all ... a medical visit as promised!
Upon arriving in Spain, I went to the Generalismo Francisco Franco General Hospital for my periodic blood test.

When the technician read my results, he panicked. "You should be in hospital!" he told me with his arms in the air, "Your white cell count is 30,000 mm^3!"

I told him I was perfectly aware of my medical situation and despite my count, I felt perfectly well.

I ended up leaving with the blessing of the doctor who reassured me I was fine.

-The big city of Madrid!
Here we were in the big city of Madrid, with its fountains, its large public squares, its parks and museums. We visited the Prado Museum and the Royal Palace.

I was blown away by so much beauty, elegance and ... opulence!
From Madrid, Earl and I went to visit Toledo and its historic synagogues, then on to Salamanca.

All evidence showed the Spaniards are very mindful of their history and religious traditions. We were also able to make a trip to the south to see Seville, Torremolinos and Grenada.

Assessment of my trip
For the young adult that I was, this trip was very enriching.

I was very impressed to walk in these Biblical places that I had studied about in books.

This trip brought history to life. It opened my eyes on the world and on the life of people far away. I caught the bug for traveling and I said to myself that I would do anything to travel as much as possible in the future.

Thanks to my parents.

Evidently, I came back with my heart full

not only of marvelous images,

but also of gratitude for my parents.

I know they would have loved to come there with me

but ... it was I, the lucky one! Thank you! Thank you!

UPON RETURNING FROM ISRAEL, AN "ALMOST" NORMAL LIFE

-My white cell count rises...
Since returning from this big voyage at the beginning of August, 1978, my white cells continued to multiply dangerously. Despite this, I was living normally.

-I want to pursue my studies.
My desire was still to become a translator. I therefore tried again to get into translation at L'Université de Montréal. However, they ruled that I still didn't meet the basic requirements.

So, I looked elsewhere. I had heard about a new Bachelor's program at L'Université du Québec à Montréal in "tourism management". I then made an application and I was accepted for the winter semester, which was going to begin in January, 1979. I therefore had off the whole autumn session.

-I look for work until returning to school.
Since I wasn't studying before winter, I found a couple of temporary jobs.

Firstly, I was a clerk at a Miracle Mart store. My work consisted of filling shelves with merchandise ... I didn't last too long there.

I quickly found a better job at the Grand Motel on Chemin de la Côte de Liesse in Saint-Laurent.

I really liked working at the front desk because I was in contact with the public.

Bernard Gotlieb organizes a Côte St. Luc tournament that attracts players from New York and Boston (The Gazette, Monday, May 31, 1982)

Founding "my" Scrabble® Club
I love the game of Scrabble® so much that I decided I would found my own club. I therefore wrote to the company Selchow & Righter (owners of Scrabble®) to ask them how one goes about forming a club.

-Scrabble® takes on more and more prominence in my life.
This company sent me the list of players who subscribed to the monthly Scrabble® newsletter. They recommended I contact Joel Wapnick, a music professor at McGill University and famous Scrabble® player who had recently moved to Montreal. I called him and he invited me to play at his home where he easily crushed me!

In autumn, 1978, I founded my Scrabble® club: we would meet twice a month at Concordia University.

A few years later, I asked club members to move closer to me at a Côte St. Luc park. In 1984 we moved to our permanent home, Trudeau Park.

It was the occasion to meet players of all levels who were looking for a challenge. I was the director of the club and it was I who organized the games.

-What a great activity Scrabble® is!
For me, Scrabble® was more than a game: it was an intellectual discipline and also a charming social activity.

Through the years I made a lot of friends: I also met all kinds of people and many who surprised me with their fascination for rare words.

-Scrabble® allows me to travel!
Scrabble® allowed me to travel: I attended through the years annual and biennial tournaments in big cities like Atlanta, Boston, New York, Reno, Cincinnati and Providence.

For me, these tournaments represented mini-vacations; I derived a lot of pleasure and satisfaction. I also participated in several weekend tournaments in Toronto, Kingston, Albany, Lake George, Saratoga and Boston. Since founding my club, I organized an annual tournament here in Montreal. We attract about 60 players from all over.

…And it helps me keep my spirits up and my heart warm.
I didn't memorize the dictionary as certain experts have done, but I adore Scrabble® just the same.

And through the trials and tribulations of my health that life has presented me, it helped me keep my spirits up and my heart warm as did the friends with whom I played and who, as you will see later on, would bring me great pleasure by coming to play with me at different hospitals that I was in over the years.

THE BONE MARROW TRANSPLANT

In December, 1978, my white cell count was around 70 000/mm^3.

-We must go to Boston to consult a specialist
Dr. Caplan asked my parents to bring me to the Sydney Farber Institute in Boston for a consultation with Dr. George P. Cannelos, specialist in the treatment of leukemia, with whom he had planned an appointment for February 9th at 9:00 a.m.

-The consultation in Boston is cancelled: urgent hospitalization!

The evening of February 7 at 10:30 p.m., while we were getting ready to leave for Boston, Dr. Caplan called our house to say that the visit to Boston would have to be postponed. This was due to the results of my blood test taken the day before which indicated, in effect, that my white blood cells had risen to $113,000/mm^3$ (blast crisis) and that my platelets had gone down by 50%. My spleen was also enlarged, a sign that the disease…was in full force!

Dr. Caplan had discussed my case with Dr. Cannelos and both doctors agreed that it was necessary at first to try to reduce my white cells to $10,000/mm^3$ or less, which would have been less dangerous.

-At the hospital for chemotherapy

Dr. Caplan told me instead to present myself to the Jewish General Hospital at 8:30 the next morning! I therefore entered this hospital where they were going to take care of me for a few days with chemotherapy medications taken orally and by injection.

-The hospital: an awkward experience!

This was the first time I was hospitalized since my childhood! As a young boy, I was in for a couple of minor operations.

This time I really felt out of place: me, a man of 20 years, full of enthusiasm and plans, what was I doing in the hospital?
My family and friends came to visit me, looking concerned. They brought me magazines, chocolates and all sorts of goodies. It was truly bizarre: I surely did not appear to be sick! The whole scenario seemed totally unreal!

I must admit that I found my situation rather comfortable. Those six days in the hospital in a semi-private room with a roommate who was very sympathetic – it was a vacation!

-A successful treatment
What's more is that I noted that Dr. Caplan had made the right choice in hospitalizing me, because in so doing, my leukemia was easier to control. He succeeded in reducing my immature white cell count from $113,000/mm^3$ to $3,000/mm^3$ with light chemotherapy. He preferred that the count even be below the norm.

-Return home after six days in the hospital
For the next four months following this hospital stay, from February to June, 1979, my head felt heavy and a bit dizzy. Dr. Caplan took regular blood tests and two bone marrow biopsies.

When the technicians took my blood, I couldn't look, so as to avoid feeling weak…I am hemaphobic (what a pretty word for Scrabble®, but what a lousy condition!).

As for my biopsies, they were more painful despite the fact that they would freeze me at the site where they took a small bone sample, generally under the pelvis. In fact, I was above all afraid of the sight of blood.

-A hope: the bone marrow transplant!
Meanwhile, my sister Gloria - who always protected me and who was always ready to do anything for me - had sought information on leukemia and available treatments. She had written to different hospitals and medical centers. By so doing, she learned that they were working on medical research in the United States to treat leukemia: the bone marrow transplant.
The treatment consisted of transplanting the bone marrow of a compatible person into the patient. By doing the bone marrow transplant, the healthy cells injected into the patient, colonized the bone marrow and took the place of cancerous cells.

Gloria then contacted Dr. Caplan to see if it were possible for me to be treated this way. The doctor assured her that he would research this treatment to see if it would work in my case; he was of the opinion that I would be able to pull through given my good physical condition.

-A difficult option for me

Should I throw myself into this adventure? It was I and I alone who had to make this decision: if I agreed and found a bone marrow donor, Dr. Caplan would arrange everything with the Toronto hospital.

It was first of all necessary to make the explicit request and for me to sign. Then, the process would be underway.

This treatment, which was in an experimental stage, represented my only hope.

For my part, I had read an article in Reader's Digest in which a Quebec dentist describes his transplant he had received that was successful in Seattle.

It was as if Damocles' sword were at my neck

The procedure cost the Quebec government the modest sum of $100,000 U.S. at the time! Since then, the government no longer assumed the cost to do it there.

It was obviously prohibitive for us.

-Dr. Caplan finds the hospital where this "experimental" treatment is being done
For his part, Dr. Caplan was doing his investigations. He discovered a Canadian medical center where the same treatment was being done, but in an experimental way, at the Princess Margaret Hospital in Toronto.

Following numerous steps, he found me a way to be treated there thanks to a reciprocity agreement between La Régie de l'Assurance Maladie du Québec (known as RAMQ or the Quebec Health Insurance Plan) and the Ontario Hospital Insurance Plan (OHIP).
I was therefore admissible for the transplant!

My parents and I discussed the transplant with Dr. Caplan. He strongly encouraged me to undergo the treatment: he assured me that everything would be for the best. It was, however, necessary to expect certain minor inconveniences, like… a few skin problems. The future would show that this was the understatement of the century!

-The biggest decision of my whole life   …
It was as if Damocle's sword were at my neck. It was a matter of choosing between on one hand, risking an experimental treatment which at worst could have unsuspected negative effects despite the hope that I could see otherwise in the future… and on the other hand, remaining in the present state I was in, knowing very well that remission would not last too long.

Notwithstanding, if the leukemia reappeared and I went out of remission, I was given 10 months to live; but who could assure me that the transplant would succeed for me? I couldn't decide.

-Once again it's the family who saves me… emotionally
In the meantime, some of my mother's cousins arrived from Cincinnati with their 3 children to spend a few days in Montreal. The father, Dr. Marvin Pravda, was a psychiatrist and his wife Myra was a nurse clinician.

I accompanied my cousins around a bit and inevitably we discussed the dilemma I was in. Both of them, with a lot of consideration, encouraged me to take the risk of the transplant considering that it was my surest hope.

I also had a lot of encouragement from my immediate family.

-I make my choice: I will launch myself into the unknown!
I met the 4 conditions for being eligible for the bone marrow transplant:

>1 - be young enough to be able to withstand the bad effects of chemotherapy;

>2 - not have received too much chemotherapy;

>3 - be in remission;

>4 - have a compatible donor.

Did I think at that moment that it was possible that I die?

I must admit that the idea crossed my mind, but in fact, I was thinking a lot more of the needles and the injections that would be awaiting me there!

-Who will be the bone marrow donor?
All my family members were willing to be tested!

It turned out that only Gloria had a compatible blood with mine. It was 90%. Her blood group was type A universal.

-Gloria has therefore won the big prize!
Happily, Gloria remained committed to giving me her blood and bone marrow. She really wanted to help her brother but it was necessary to do it as soon as possible before becoming pregnant with her second child, as she had planned.

Dr. Caplan's dedication
Dr. Caplan made all the arrangements as he had promised. He worked for me as whole-heartedly as professionally. He wasn't asking me to go: he was ordering me to go!

Preparations for leaving for the Princess Margaret Hospital
Happily, right up until my departure for Toronto, I didn't have the time to twiddle my thumbs: I was leaving with my mother. We had to pack our bags and above all, plan out our stay in Toronto.

JUNE 19, 1979 TO TORONTO
TO RECEIVE MY SISTER GLORIA'S BONE MARROW

-Getting settled in Toronto
Having arrived in Toronto via Air Canada, my mother and I were only able to stay 3 days at the downtown Carlton Inn because they were full.

We then had to find another lodging for the rest of my hospitalization, which isn't easy to do in Toronto.

We were looking for the closest lodging to the Princess Margaret Hospital so that the family could be close to me during my treatment. A friend had recommended an affordable hotel which was close to the hospital. We went to see it.

The hotel was called the "Waldorf Astoria"! It was the name they dared to call this efficiency which, at first sight, seemed not very recommendable. It was inhabited by the Vietnamese boat people who the Canadian government had taken in as immigrants. The hotel seemed to be in a deplorable state.

Nevertheless, the suite that we visited seemed to be clean: there was one separate bedroom, a living room with a hide-a-bed and a kitchenette. This seemed to suit us. We would move in 3 days later.

The same day we arrived in Toronto, we went to the Princess Margaret Hospital, also known as the Ontario Cancer Institute.

-The compatibility test between Gloria's blood and mine
I brought to Toronto the blood sample that Dr. Caplan had taken from Gloria before leaving Montreal, as well as my medical history. They took a blood sample from me, then mixed our 2 bloods in a test tube: they would have to be watched for a week to see if they could live together without one attacking the other. If this indeed occurred, it would have to be determined which of the 2 bloods were attacking the other.

-The bone marrow test
The next day, Wednesday afternoon, we walked to the hospital where I was to undergo a bone marrow test. We then met Dr. Curtis, one of the 2 doctors of the team of specialists.

He was very nice. His voice was soft, calming and his warm smile reassured me. He explained to me the whole procedure in detail.

Then, I, left the hospital again with my hospital pass, "as an external patient, for a few more days" as Dr. Curtis put it.

-On vacation in Toronto … as an external patient until June 21
I was therefore still on vacation in Toronto! I was happy about it. We were, my mother and I, tourists with, however, a heavy heart.

We went to the CN Tower, and then at night my cousin-in-law Dave Friedman came to bring us to his place. We were received by my cousin Judy, his wife, along with her newborn, little Beth. I will always be able to later on calculate Beth's age: she was born in April, 1979 just about 2 months before the transplant.

-My official admission to the Princess Margaret Hospital!
Thursday, June 21, 1979 was supposed to be the day of my official admission to the hospital. I was ready. I presented myself, somewhat apprehensive, with my mother to admissions.

-Concern among the medical team: a postponement
A doctor from the medical team came to warn us that the transplant would be delayed until July because preparations were more complicated than originally predicted.

So I swallowed my emotions and tried to go back to my vacation spirit! I must say I was mixed with my feelings: I had total confidence in the doctors on the medical team, but I knew that the treatment was still in its experimental phase. I tried to convince myself that all would succeed.

My sister Gloria, whom I reached by phone seemed, like me, both concerned but still full of hope.

In the afternoon my mother and I, like good tourists, went to the Eaton Center, an enormous shopping center in the heart of the city.

-My father comes to join us
Learning that we had another week off, my dad came out the same day to join us in Toronto. I let him use my bed at the hotel while I went to sleep at the hospital, since my room had been reserved for me there.

The next day we went for a drive and visited Chinatown. At night, my father and I went for a walk on Yonge Street near the hotel, for a little "man-to-man" talk.

-Second postponement! A patient on reprieve …
Friday, June 22nd, we finally met at length with the eminent Dr. Hans Messner, a young, nice, serious and very conscientious man. I felt confident that he was my main doctor hematologist.

He answered our numerous questions with patience. Then he underlined the gravity of my case and added that it would still be necessary to wait another week to proceed.

I was a little bit worried.

-The vacation … continues with the family
On the weekend, my sister Sharon came to join us from Ottawa, where she taught French. We did a whole bunch of activities, including a visit to the famous Science Museum of Ontario. Sunday night we went to my cousins Judy and Dave's house for "The Last Supper".

This meal was really out of the ordinary. We appreciated every moment together.
Coming back from the hotel, I had to gather all my stuff because I was going into the hospital for real the next morning.

I had received flowers from my Aunt Evelyn, from our neighbours the Weinsteins, and from my mother's friend Anita.

I did not expect such niceness: as I didn't feel sick, I found it rather funny that I was being so spoiled.

JUNE 1979, THE PREPARATORY MONTH

JUNE 1979, THE PREPRATORY MONTH

Monday, June 25th, 1979, was the actual day of my admittance to the Princess Margaret Hospital. This time, it was serious. Tourism was over for me.

-"A procedure which is not without risk": I have to sign ...
They did tests on me.

Dr. Messner once again explained the procedure, underlined the risks that I would run and asked me again for my written consent. Obviously, I couldn't go back. I signed.

... And to keep up my morale
As for myself – I still felt very much fit and healthy – I was wondering what I was getting myself into…

Everything seemed unreal.

Circumstances showed me the unconditional love of my family.

While leaving Toronto, my sister Sharon was crying…

The whole family was worried and I saw the effort that each one was doing to keep smiling in front of me.

-My hospital room
The patient with whom I would share my room was Meford Thompson. He also suffered from leukemia. He was a man of 62 years, kind and quiet: he came from the small community of Barry, in Ontario. We had good conversations together.

We felt pampered: only the 2 of us in a big room with a bathroom for us alone. We had a big window (we should have escaped!), except that the view was unexciting: it was the hospital wall. Happily, we had a television and our interests were the same.

-Unfortunately, it is necessary to eat ...

The only negative point for me was the food. Like a student who every day does his homework, I had to tick off the food I wanted. If I wanted something else, all I had to do was to write it at the bottom of the menu. As I am a difficult eater, I was always afraid to try new plates. The hospital is not a place for gastronomic adventures!

-And, to see blood again!

A nurse used to come once or twice a day with a big needle to administer chemotherapy by injection to Meford ... She would pull the curtain around him so I couldn't see anything: I am so afraid of needles and blood! I said to myself that one day, it would be me going through that.

-A preparatory lumbar puncture

At first, Dr. Messner came to see me. He did a lumbar puncture test on me to extract a bit of vertebral fluid. This supplementary test was necessary to ensure that everything would go well. It could thus verify if any leukemic cells had invaded my spine or not. He also installed an intravenous line through which he would later inject chemotherapy.

After this lumbar puncture, I had to remain flat on my back for 6 hours to avoid getting a migraine. I ate my meal in this position: I challenge anyone to swallow a steak like that! Then, I stayed still hoping the test would result in good news.

-The sky darkens: the medical team's new hesitation

The medical team considered itself finally ready to treat me. However, this time the problem was coming from the patient! In effect, the day after the lumbar puncture, they came to inform me that they found leukemic cells in my spine...

-They are thinking of sending me back to Montreal...

This was a real setback! Five leukemic patients had all died before me of pneumonia following their bone marrow transplant... to such a point that the doctors thought it was plausible to completely stop the procedure and to send me back to Montreal.

-The medical team decides to proceed… just the same…
The medical team wanted to yet again delay the transplant until the end of July: they feared that they couldn't give me chemotherapy and radiation at the same time. Nevertheless, as the radiologist insisted, it was decided to proceed just the same according to the original plan of July 5th, given that everything was already set to go for a while.

Preparations were under way.

Now I looked like a real patient

University Health Network

BONE MARROW TPANSPLANT PROTOCOL FOR MR. BERNARD GOTLIEB

BACKGROUND INFORMATION:
Mr. Bernard Gotlieb is a 20 year old white male with Philadelphia positive CML. He was initially diagnosed in February of 1978 and remained asymptomatic without any font of treatment until February 1979.

At that time he was found to be in blastosis with'a WBC count exceeding 100,000. Morphologicaliy, the blast cells displayed features of a lymphoblastic leukemia.

He responded well to treatment with Vincristine and Prednisone, and being in remission was transferred for bone marrow transplantation. Additional investigation reveals his CSF positive for blast cells.

His preconditioning regimen will include cranial radiation and intrathecal injections with cytosine arabinoside, L-asparaginase, Vincristine Prednisone, cyclophosphamide and 500 rads total body radiation. He wiil receive the bone narrow transplant from his HLA-identica1 MLR non-responsive sister Gloria.

Princess Margaret Hospital

THE IMMEDIATE PREPARATION FOR THE TRANSPLANT

-A worrisome decision…
The postponement of the treatment was for me more troubling than for the medical team – who we knew – were looking for successes, or at least partial successes, to maintain their financing from the government. It was therefore necessary to seek out successes…

I was thus to become an experimental guinea pig, someone they'd learn from…

-My head is used as a target!
The same day, the nurse Cathy – charming like all the others – came to see me with a pair of scissors to cut my hair. She wanted to shave my head.

Obviously, I wasn't thrilled… She explained to me that, in any event, with the chemotherapy, I would lose my hair…

I calmed down and she cut my hair with the scissors as short as she could. Later on, Kim, a Korean nurse – also very nice but more determined – came in to finish the job with a real razor on my skull! I felt naked on my head: I was cold up there!

Maureen Harlick, an older nurse who was very kind and sympathetic with motherly care put a light blue bonnet on my head… but it was nonetheless heavy for the morale.

-Now I look like a real patient!
I looked in the mirror in the bathroom and I no longer wanted to see myself nor be seen: it was dreadful. Horrible!

When my mother and Gloria saw me, they told me I looked fine. Obviously, they were trying to console me, but I'm sure they also had a shock.

Then, the radiologist came to draw on my head: he traced lines to mark out where they would radiate. He explained to me that for the next 5 days they were going to radiate me for one minute on each side of the head.

-Preparation for the radiation
The same day, June 26th, I had to go down to the radiation department for the first time. My dad accompanied me. We waited for more than an hour which I found very difficult, given the anxiety I was feeling.

Finally, I went into the room and they had me stretch out on a table where the technician lowered a kind of giant funnel to one side of my head in order to release the radiation. She then placed a kind of plate on the other side to block the radiation there.

Following that, she went out of the room and left me alone.
Very alone.

-The first radiation session
I had no idea what to expect. I did not want to look. Really, I was scared. I thus received for the first time a minute of radiation, first to the left side of my head and then to the right side.

-A burning smell
At first I heard a noise, then I smelled something like a burnt hot-dog which made me a bit nauseous.

The train left the station! And I thought I was being run over…

-The second radiation session
The next day I received the second dose of radiation, then they started giving me chemotherapy through the i.v. in my arm. The dermatologist took a skin biopsy from a little section of my chest that he had frozen.

Since the beginning of these radiation sessions, I was nauseous and didn't want to eat. I stayed in bed the whole day.

They gave me very powerful drugs to destroy all my white cells and at the same time destroy all my leukemic cells.

-Other compatibility tests on Gloria and me
Gloria had arrived in Toronto on June 25th. She was admitted to the hospital for the night of June 27th.

To assure that everything would go right, the doctors wanted once again to test Gloria and my blood's' compatibility.

-The cell-separator machine
For even more assuredness, they further tested our compatibility by other means: they installed a catheter in each of Gloria's arms which hooked up to a cell-separator machine. My sister's red cells went into one bag; her white cells into another.

This machine is selective and only takes from the donor the blood that the patient needs. In my case, the cell-separator would retain Gloria's white cells through one arm and return the rest of the blood to her through the other arm. The whole thing took 2 ½ hours.

Happily, the results of the test were excellent: our blood-types were compatible. Encouraging news!

-Gloria returns to Montreal after the compatibility tests
That evening, Gloria and my Dad retuned to Montreal. I could just imagine what they were talking about.

I was imagining that my father would have liked to stay on. However, as he was a plumber and had to take care of his plumbing shop, he had to return to work. He toiled hard for his family, but never did I hear him complain about his responsibilities.

-Always, the sight of blood!
When Dr. Messner had installed the intravenous, I didn't want to move my arm for the next 5 to 6 days for fear of it blocking up! I know that was a little exaggerated, but I was so worried: this long needle that they put into my flesh- it was horrible for me! I always hoped it would run well.

To relieve my nausea, a side effect of the chemotherapy, they gave me a medication the next day.

Once, there was a problem: blood was spurting from my arm because the i.v. came out: I became weak: I can't stand the sight of blood. Above all – my own!

What is ironic in my adventure is that all this treatment has to do with blood and that since my childhood; the sight of blood weakens me!

Up until that point, everything was going fine.

-Two other radiation sessions
Friday, June 29 was the 4th radiation treatment to my head. I also received my chemotherapy treatment. Following that, interns Kerr and Goldberg did a lumbar puncture on me.

-They install a subclavian line
Dr. Messner and nurse Eunice came next to insert, under local anesthetic, a subclavian line which was to replace the intravenous in my arm. This was done in order to save my veins and also free my arms.

When the effect of the anesthetic wore off, I began to have pain: I wasn't yet used to this uncomfortable apparatus. That night, I had nausea.

-This subclavian – finally, what relief!
This new apparatus allowed me to go on hyper-alimentation: all necessary nutrients passed through this subclavian. I no longer had to fill out menus nor eat. Marvelous! One less chore!

This subclavian was the best thing that happened to me. It constituted a direct line from the jugular vein to the heart. Once installed, it could last up to a month and a half. Evidently, it had to be kept sterile and carefully cleaned.

I had to nevertheless get used to these tubes which were coming out of me. It was rather cumbersome, it's true.

-Last radiation before isolation
Saturday, June 30th was my last radiation treatment to the head: I was ready to leave my room to enter the isolation room – 534, the other side of the hall.

-The serious adventure is about to begin…
Dallas, a particularly efficient, sweet and pretty nurse, came to prepare me for the necessary sterilization for the isolation period. She gave me a bath with a disinfectant soap and then she put a white, sterile robe on me. Even though I was fully capable of walking, she made me sit in the wheelchair. She pushed me at full speed, to avoid germs, towards the isolation room where I would have to stay until the end of the transplant.

THE ISOLATION ROOM

My new room was very pleasant: medium size, it had a few windows overlooking an alleyway and from where I could see a little church. Fresh air was circulating well to keep the room sterile. It was even cool enough that I sometimes had to ask for an additional blanket.

The room was well-stocked, well-designed: I had an electric bed which allowed me to change positions by myself without anyone's help. I had a TV without a remote control however, which obliged me to bother someone to open it, close it or change channels… me who hates to bother people.

Also found in my room were all sorts of supplies and medical apparatus. I had in addition, for me alone, a bathroom with a shower and a bathtub.

-A strict procedure to be respected by visitors
In this isolation room I could receive visitors, but they had to respect a meticulous procedure. Every visitor had to be well asepticized before entering my room.

-Each visitor has to adhere to the following orders:
     1- don a gown;
     2- put on a mask over the mouth;
     3- wear a bonnet on the head;
     4- slip on paper shoe covers;
     5- wash their hands well with a sterilizing soap;
     6- slip on gloves.

If the visitor stayed more than an hour in my room, they'd have to change their mask.

MARVELLOUS NURSES

The nurses were not only efficient, but were warm and very compassionate. They were precious: they were my rays of sunshine! They were trained to work with patients suffering from cancer.

All the nurses were attentive to my needs. One night for example, I was unable to sleep because Meford was snoring too loudly. I asked for help from Minnie, an Indian nurse; she found me another room for the night. She didn't say it then, but it was to be the isolation room reserved for me.

Alice, also an Indian, was very warm and very sympathetic. When she came into our room with her long needle to give Mr. Thompson chemotherapy, she always had a big smile on her face, which helped us be more relaxed. She always outdid herself to find the way to comfort me and to make life easier. There was also Eunice, another exceptional nurse, full of life, loquacious, alive and passionate about astrology. Another, Maureen, was very pretty and I used to love teasing her. The head nurse Ingrid was also always in good humour and used to laugh with me. It was wonderful for me to be in contact with all these nurses, as kind as they were competent.

-My life in this isolation room
To tell the truth, the days spent in my isolation room were not unpleasant.

First of all, I was no longer inconvenienced by having to eat meals since I was on hyperalimentation: I was receiving nourishment through my subclavian, which was for me, paradise! I no longer had to get dressed and undressed every day since I was always in a hospital gown.

To stay in shape, I had to move a bit: I used to walk in my room from one wall to the other, about a dozen feet, at least 20 times a day. My subclavian line was always attached, but the wires were long enough to allow me to exercise.

I kept myself quite busy: I was able to watch TV and listen to the radio. Too bad I am not a reader: I never had the patience to sit down with a book…

I often used to call my mother at the hotel to find out what was doing, who had called her or who would be coming to visit me. When my father arrived in Toronto, he would come up and read me the get-well cards I received (250 in all! hung up in my room). We would do crossword puzzles together.

JULY '79, THE NEXT FATEFUL MONTH

Sunday, July 1, I still had a lot of nausea and I was suffering from a constant diarrhea which was very humiliating: I hated dirtying my gowns and the bed. I was embarrassed by the chore I was imposing on the nurses, but they took care of everything with patience and kindness.

-The last preparations
On Monday, July 2, they did another lumbar puncture: I was already used to it now and I knew I had to stay flat on my back without moving for six hours. Tuesday morning, I felt sick but I was able to play two games of Scrabble with my mother. My father also returned to Toronto. I was happy to see him close to me.

-Gloria's admission to the hospital
As for Gloria, she was once again admitted to the hospital. They gave her room 419E on the fourth floor. They avoided placing a donor and recipient on the same floor.

-Thursday, July 5, 1979: total body radiation
At 6:30 in the morning, they came to get me in my isolation room and covered me from head to toe, then stretched me out straight on the stretcher.
It was the first time before the transplant that I went out of the isolation room: they would bring me right back after the treatment. A stretcher-bearer rolled me at full speed to the radiation room which is in the hospital basement. Once there, I was transferred onto a very low bed near the floor. I had to stay still and flat on my back while they put sandbags between my thighs in order to protect me from the radiation. Then they left me alone…

As I didn't know what to expect, I was feeling a big fear on the inside.

They lowered an immense machine on me. I closed my eyes. They told me that I would be notified after two and a half minutes, which was half the treatment.

I was going to receive total body radiation: 500 rads, five minutes to the front side and then five minutes to the back side. This was to be, after a week or so of heavy chemotherapy, the final blow to completely destroy my immune system and obliterate my bone marrow which was producing leukemic cells.

-Again the smell of burnt hot-dogs...
When the radiation was released, I heard a hissing sound and once again I smelled that burnt hot-dog smell coming from the machine...

After the radiation on one side, the nurses turned me on my stomach. Again the sandbags were placed between my thighs before the nurses went out.

Fortunately I didn't feel any nausea during the treatment. When the nurses lifted me up to go back on the stretcher however, I had to ask for a basin because of nausea, but I was unable to vomit despite my efforts. They brought me back to my isolation room at top speed by stretcher.

The side effects of the five minutes of radiation were going to affect me the rest of my life!

MY SISTER GLORIA'S BONE MARROW DONATION

-Gloria's bone marrow donation
The same day, Gloria went into the operating room. Under general anesthetic, they made 25 little cuts around the sternum and hips to extract bone marrow.

They then inserted 220 suction needles into her. They filled a bag of her marrow (like blood). The whole process took two and a half hours...

Following that, Dr. Messner ran down the hall carrying the three bags of my sister's bone marrow. My father, my mother, Sharon, Fred and Gordon (Gloria's husband) were able to watch through a window in my room which had open curtains.

My mother wrote in her diary that day: "What a sacrifice did she do for her brother! May God bless Gloria! You can't buy this bone marrow for all the money in the world… She is proud to be able to give a new life to her brother."

-As for me…
As for me, I was not able, alas, to look at this bone marrow, nevertheless so desired, because of my horror at seeing blood: I had to ask that they cover up the bag on the i.v. pole!

-My sister's bone marrow is given to me by transfusion
Gloria's bone marrow was transfused into me by my subclavian. This subclavian was also for me a good and easy way of receiving my medications.

During these transfusions, Dr. Messner monitored my blood pressure and heartbeat.

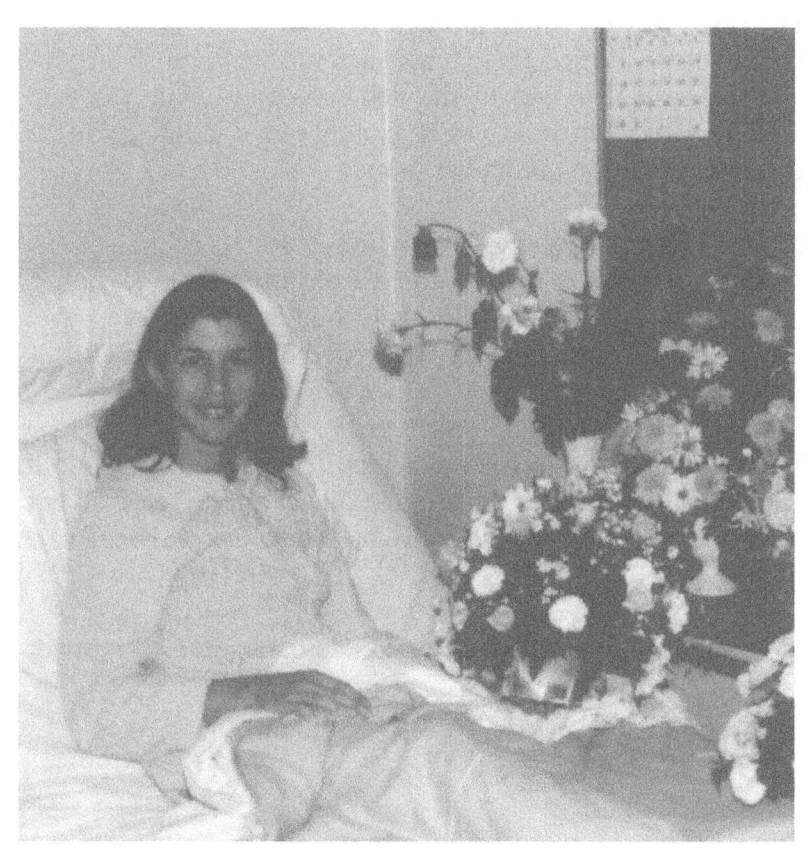

My sister Gloria

-Gloria's first and second day on the cell-separator
Friday morning, July 6, Gloria went on the cell-separator to give white cells. The plan called for her to do this for three hours for five days in a row.

The second day, after her three hour session she felt weaker and dizzier.

-The third day on the machine
Gloria got up from her bed, took a few steps and then got dizzy. She was helped to get to the cell-separator. She did her three hours, however, the task was becoming more and more difficult for her to bear and was taxing her morale.

-Gloria's fourth day of giving white cells
Monday morning, Gloria returned from the fourth session in pain and feeling miserable. After only one hour, she was overcome with dizziness. She asked for the procedure to be stopped.

-Gloria is exhausted: she must stop
The doctor gave her some medication intravenously to soothe her. Seeing her white and in a state of exhaustion, he released her from the famous machine saying to her: "You can stop. You've earned your medal!"

It was very good: my dear sister had demonstrated a lot of courage.

Waldorf Astoria Hotel
80 - 88 CHARLES ST. EAST
TORONTO, ONTARIO M4Y 1V4
923-3581

White Cell Donors

Tuesday, July 10th	①	Sharon	✓
Wed, July 11th	①	Gordon	✓
Thurs, July 12th	①	Freddie	✓
Fri, July 13th	①	Manny	✓
Sat, July 14th	①	Dave Friedman	✓
Sun, July 15th	②	Sharon (10 a.m.)	✓
Mon, July 16th	①	Gladys (9 p.m.)	✓
Tues, July 17th	①	Murray Dubarsky	✓
Wed, July 18th	②	Freddie	✓
Thurs, July 19th	①	Elaine Belanger (Esther's friend) 10p	✓
Fri, July 20th	②	Murray Dubarsky	
Sat, July 21st	②	Dan Friedman (1:00 p.m.)	✓
Sun, July 22nd	①	Morrie Zucker	✓
Mon, July 23rd	②	Manny	✓

-Other white cell donors must take over
After Gloria's contributions, it was necessary to find other donors for the next two weeks: I needed white cells since my count was practically zero.

My sister Sharon took charge of finding relatives and volunteers whose blood was compatible to mine, so that I could receive their white cells from the cell-separator (I needed white cells until Gloria's bone marrow would take root and produce healthy white cells).

Her friend, Esther Blum, who was living in Toronto, helped her with this task.

-Family and friends participate in my rescue!
Fortunately I was able to once again count on my large family for my rescue.

Among the generous donors, there were the following:
- my father: 33,000 and 34,000 white cells;
- my sister Sharon: 11,000 and 20,000;
- my brother Fred: 28,000 and 33,500;
- my Uncle Murray: 65,000 then 63,000;
- my Aunt Gladys: 28,000 and 35,000;
- Gordon: 35,000;
- my cousin David Friedman: 10,000 and 26,000;
- Esther's friend Elaine Belanger: 45,000;
- and a very nice student from York University, Morrie Zucker 22,000.

```
                          white cells
David J.         1) 10,000
Gordon           2) 26,000
              →  1) 55,000
Fred             1) 28,500
                 2) 33,500
Dad              1) 33,000
                 2) 34,000
Sharon           1) 11,000
                 2) 20,000
Gladys           1) 75,000
Murray           1) 65,000
                 2) 63,000
Elaine           1) 45,000
Morris           1) 22,000
```

-For me, every time, the same procedure
After each blood donation, a nurse entered my room to do the transfusion. Every time she would ask me my name and my patient number. I found this funny, but this was the protocol!

-Obviously, certain "side effects"…
As for me, during the whole time I was receiving blood I spiked a fever. I had constant shivers and headaches. Often I'd go from being so cold, needing a blanket, to so hot and burning up. My mouth was dry, without saliva and full of ulcers. My taste buds weren't working either. They gave me something to suck on that was moist in order to keep my mouth a little wet.

I had some serious bedsores… that were healed thanks to three sitz baths a day, thus avoiding infection which could have been serious in my case.

MY SISTER GLORIA'S OWN ACCOUNT

I will never forget that day! My father had arrived at my house in Montreal, his face strained by emotion. He seemed very upset. In trying to find his words, he told me that my brother Bernard was suffering from leukemia.

I think this was the worst moment of my life. It was a cruel announcement: Bernard was only 19 years old: he had his whole life ahead of him.

As I am his older sister by eight years and our family is very close, I couldn't just sit there and do nothing to help him. I felt that I got the calling: I had to find the way to save Bernard's life. This came as an urgent call.

For me, it was the beginning of a distressful period: I couldn't get Bernard out of my mind. I wrote letters to different hospitals throughout the world specializing in cancer, asking them at what stage they were in treating this blood cancer. To my pleasant surprise, I was sent documentation on a new experimental procedure which was called "the bone marrow transplant".

Proud of my discovery, I spoke about it to Dr. Caplan, Bernard's hematologist at the Jewish General Hospital. I asked him if I could give my bone marrow to my brother.

The doctor, however, curbed my enthusiasm by telling me that we first of all had to take compatibility tests in the family to see who would be the ideal donor.

Not long after, when the tests were done, I received a phone call from Dr. Caplan. The results showed that I would be the ideal donor: Our blood was totally compatible. The doctor asked me if I still wanted to volunteer. I answered "Certainly! I want to!"

The necessary steps for doing a bone marrow transplant could now begin. It would be the beginning of the rest of Bernard's life!

Then, the day of the transplant…
Waking up after having given the bone marrow, I felt sharp, shooting pains in the areas where they took bone marrow: the sternum and above the hips.

Afterwards, in order to help in the success of the transplant, I started to give white cells. To do this, they hooked me up to a cell-separator machine twice a day. After four days, however, I had become very weak: I needed a blood transfusion…

During this whole time, I never stopped praying for a minute.

Thirty years later, I look back and feel the rush of emotions I experienced and shared with my family.

Now, I am very happy that Bernard survived so many obstacles. He is a relentless fighter. He has kept a positive attitude from the beginning. He never gave up hope of overcoming his adversities. That is why he is still among us today. He is my hero!

Gloria Gotlieb Halpern

IT'S NOW NECESSARY TO AVOID REJECTION!

-Learning to live with my sister's bone marrow,,,
Dr. Messner prescribed for me some exercises to do ten times an hour in order to prevent muscular weakness. I needed to develop the strength necessary to "digest" the graft.

What I had to do was to inhale and to exhale as deeply as possible to avoid pneumonia. Every day I had an X-ray done and, since I wasn't allowed to leave the room, the technicians had to bring the portable machine to me. For my part, I was a little worried: I suffered from a wicked headache and a bad pain on my right side.

-A peril to avoid: rejection of the graft!
The big worry for a medical team during the first 100 days following a transplant, was "graft-versus-host disease" (GVHD). Dr. Messner always maintained that it was very important to get past these first 100 critical days. I always remember my father's famous words "If only I could be five years older right now!"

-In my case, it is the graft which is attacking me, its host!
Normally in a transplant, a recipient rejects the graft (a kidney, a heart, etc.): it sees it as foreign and the recipient's immune system rejects and destroys it. Now, in my case, the graft felt totally secure: since the chemotherapy and total body radiation had destroyed my immune system, I was far from being able to attack this foreign body. Au contraire, I was the perfect prey for the intruder.

This is what is called the "graft-versus-host disease".

My antibodies became the target of the donor's graft: the bone marrow – sensing that it wasn't in the right body – was attacking my body as foreign! It could attack different organs, like the skin or lungs…

And yet how I wanted this graft! The GVHD could be acute or chronic: in my case I developed the latter that attacked primarily my skin. However, in a way they say a little GVHD is good because the body becomes so busy fighting it off, that the leukemia doesn't get a chance to come back (it's known as the GVHD-versus-leukemia effect).

-An exhausting battle!
After a week or two of receiving white blood cells and platelets, I began having some problems: in addition to my shivers and temperature rising and descending rapidly, I also had diarrhea and nausea. Then my skin began to flake.

A part of the daily routine was the taking of blood from the arm and the end of the finger. I would get a daily reading of my white cell, red cell and platelet counts.

-Enemy number one: infection
As I was unable to take a bath or shower, I was washed with a red disinfectant liquid soap which was applied to my whole body.

During all this period, I wasn't allowed to brush my teeth for fear my gums would bleed which could have evoked an infection.

So long as Gloria's bone marrow hadn't taken root in me and begin to produce white cells – it was normally a matter of a few weeks – it was necessary to be very careful for me not to be in contact with germs.

Thus, the bandages around the subclavian catheter had to be removed and disinfected every three days. As these bandages would stick to my skin, it was a bit of a painful ordeal when they'd be pulled off.

-Good news: the beginning of white cell production!
July 19, be it two weeks after the transplant, Dr. Messner had some good news to tell me after a bone marrow test: my body succeeded in producing 300 white cells!

This wasn't a lot, but it was a beginning and a good step towards autonomy. This meant that Gloria's bone marrow had finally taken root in me and she was beginning to become part of me!

-The whole family breathes a bit better!
The medical team, my mother and I were very excited. I immediately called Gloria. She was very moved and she cried... She called my father who had returned to Montreal two days earlier to tell him the good news. A friend from Ottawa called my sister Sharon.

My family was now reassured of my immediate fate. What's more, the fluid in my lungs was reducing: a sign the doctors were waiting for.

Dr. Caplan called me, all happy with my progress. He wanted to invite me to a talk he was giving in Montreal In November on bone marrow transplants! Both of us were hoping... that this would be possible!

A BIG STEP TOWARDS AUTOMONY

Normally, the doctors did their daily rounds towards the end of the afternoon. They would enter my isolation room masked and gloved. They would examine me, listen to my heart with a stethoscope and inquire about me.

My charming nurse Dallas, whom my father used to call "Texas", had told us that the day when Dr. Messner would enter my room without a gown or mask, that would be the sign that I would be let out of my isolation.

-The day so longed for
It happened July 24th! My father, masked, was with me when Dr. Messner entered my room. Upon seeing him, my father exclaimed, "But, but, doctor, you forgot your mask!"

Like a radiant sun, the good doctor said to me "Bernard, you produced 950 white cells: you no longer need to be in isolation!"

Wow! It was the day before my birthday: what an unexpected gift! I could now go out of this room and meet other people normally!

Too bad: my mother had gone out shopping with my sister Sharon.

My father was quite disappointed not being able to inform them right away. They weren't coming back to the hospital until the evening because they were going to have supper at a friend's. When they did arrive, my dad was waiting for them in the antechamber, "Enter!" he said to them, "Bernard is waiting for you."

They slipped on their gown, put on their mask and entered, followed by my father. "Relax; remove all that, I am no longer in isolation!" I said while stretching my arms out to them.
What joy it was for them! And for me! It had been so long that I was deprived of my mother's smile behind the mask she had to wear.

It had been so long that I was deprived of my mother's smile!

-My first outings in open air!
That night, I went out of the isolation room for the first time. Dallas had put a mask and gown on me! Even though I was out of danger, it was nonetheless necessary that I be careful and I go at it gradually. The best time to go out was at nighttime, because there were less people around, therefore fewer germs.

My first real outing brought me to the nurses' desk during a visit from my brother Fred. He then declared these historic words "It's one small step for Bernard and a giant step into his new life!"

The next day, July 25, 1979- my 21st birthday, my white cell counts had gone up to 1,500 and my platelets to 40 000: it was really encouraging. I was ready for a social life!

-They organize a super birthday party!
Sharon had organized a wonderful birthday party with the assistance of my parents. They had brought nuts, chocolate, alcohol and of course, a superb birthday cake that read "Happy Birthday Bernard!"

In our family everyone likes to sing, led by my dad who loves music and who is a member of the Barbershoppe choral group: The South Shore Saints.

It's too bad that I couldn't eat with the guests: I had neither the desire nor the capacity, but my pleasure was satisfied in seeing everyone happy. I received some gifts and one nurse, Joan Gould, made a donation to the volunteers in my honour.

Everyone was with me- with their whole heart.

I also had a lot of phone calls: firstly, from my sister Gloria who was very emotional, then from my cousin Harriet Terdiman, my aunts Claire and Frieda from New York, Rose, Evelyn, Gladys, Goldie, and from friends of the family: Rita Pearson, Ruth Josef and Saidie Segal…

They made me a big birthday party

-And my social life is coming back!
Now that I was no longer in isolation, I was able to go down to the hospital X-ray room with my subclavian apparatus and take some walks in the hallway, which I like to call my "walks on the moon". I still had to wear a mask and gown to be protected.

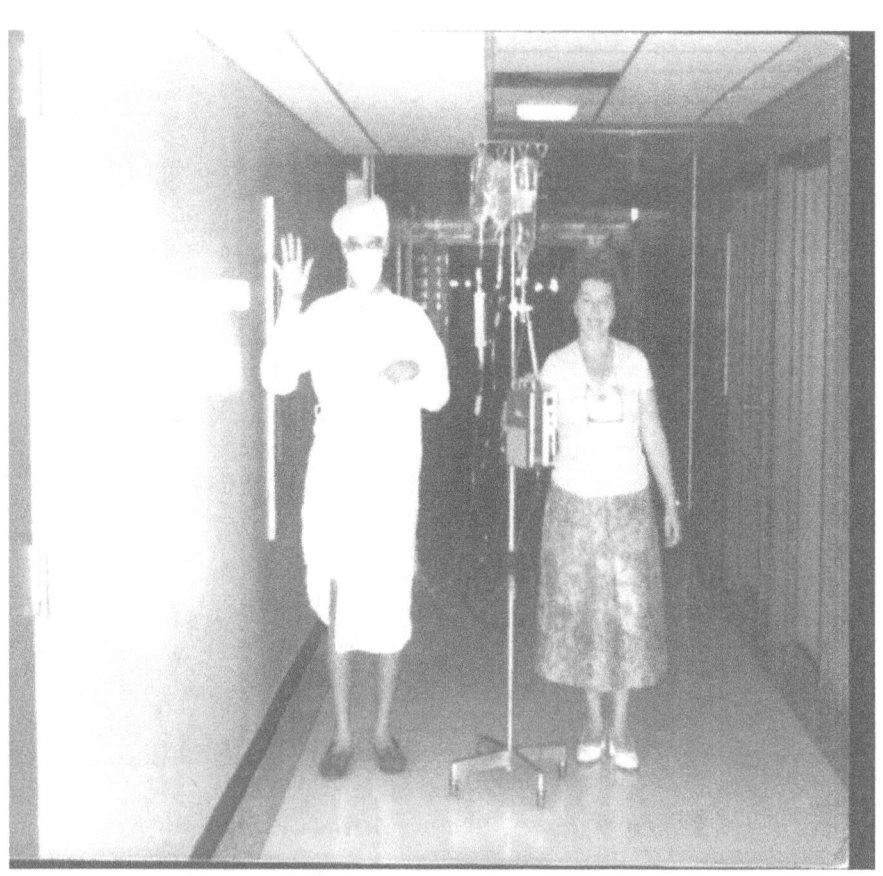

My mother and I on one of my "moonwalks" in the hallway

-Unfortunately, my poor legs abandon me…
While hoping to regain my strength and being resolved to do a lot of exercises, the very active walking became more difficult from day to day…

Once, on August 8th, 1979, I wanted to go down to the X-ray room but my legs completely abandoned me: while leaning against the wall in the hallway, I slid down towards the floor. Fortunately, Hymie Engel, my friend Earl's uncle was visiting me that day. He held me up.

The nurses then told me not to put any effort into walking. I became so weak with my legs that I couldn't even transfer from my bed to a wheelchair!

-Not any reflexes…
The next day, Drs. Curtis and Izko as well as nurses Ingrid and Maureen came to examine my legs. Realizing that I didn't have any reflexes, they called Dr. Birnbaum, a neurologist at the Wellesley Hospital, a general hospital attached to the Princess Margaret.

-Dr. Birnbaum comes to examine me
One week later, I had a myelogram test done: thanks to a dye, they were able to see if there were anything pressing on my spine. I had to stay immobile for 24 hours!

-Diagnosis: a peripheral neuropathy
The next day, Dr. Birnbaum, noting that the result was negative, deduced that this weakness known as a peripheral neuropathy, was due to nerve damage in the legs from the waist down.

-The culprit: without a doubt, Vincristine…
The doctor was of the opinion that the Vincristine they had injected into my spine to kill off the cancerous cells was the cause of this weakness. I believe that they had given me too much Vincristine: they didn't know exactly how much to give to make sure the leukemic cells were killed off in the spine (if you kill off

all the leukemic cells in the whole body but not in the spine, from the spine they would go to the head and ball game over).

Afterwards, the skin on my legs became all numb and my feet, hypersensitive. When the doctors would check the sensibility of the sole of my feet with a tuning fork, the pain was so uncontrollable that they risked having my foot end up in their mouth!
Sometimes, my legs would shake from involuntary spasms from the nerve damage, my fingers would cramp up and I'd have to physically hold them to break the painful cramps. I failed the test which consisted of distinguishing if the doctor were bending my big toe downwards or upwards. According to my doctors, I would have to wait several months before I could walk again…

-My poor hemoglobin!
Also at this time, my blood counts were not very good: they were decreasing…

Dr. Curtis believed that one of the medications I was taking, septra, was the cause of the nerve damage. He took me off it and prescribed another transfusion because my hemoglobin had decreased to 8 (normal being 15), which meant I was anemic.

-Too bad! It is necessary to start eating again…
One day, the dietician came to tell me that soon they were going to remove my subclavian line and therefore my hyper-alimentation would stop as well. This meant that I would have to start eating again.

I was doing so well in not eating! She told me that I would obviously not be able to wear that apparatus my whole life. Truthfully, I could not resign myself to having to eat again!

As the poor dietician was trying in vain to fill out my menu, she asked me to think of my favourite food that I really would like to eat. I answered her, not too enthusiastically… "Eggrolls, perhaps!" She then marked them down on my menu.

The next day, a Chinese woman who was working in the hospital kitchen came into my room all out of breath to tell me, "We no Chinese restaurant here: we have no eggrolls!"

Then the dietician came in to ask me if there were something else I would like.

I answered her while searching through my gustatory memory:

- "Perhaps cashew nuts…"
- "Okay!", she said to me.

So she left to go buy some at a nut store on the other side of the street!

I will never forget neither her kindness nor the difficult sensation I had when I tried to chew one of those nuts without saliva in my mouth…

I had not made the right choice in food with which to start eating again!

It took a few weeks before I was able to really eat!

-A serious problem of dry skin
At that moment my skin – above all, the skin on my legs – was very dry due to the radiation. I also had a very dry mouth and dry eyes.

-From the isolation room to a regular room
In mid-August, they decided to transfer me from my isolation room to a regular private room.

During this period, I used to sit in my wheelchair: I was able to go out of my room and, in so doing, change the decor. I was not, however, able to stray too far: I still had the subclavian line and had to drag a pole.

Often my mother would push my wheelchair and bring me to the end of the hallway which overlooked the street. I could thus verify that I was still part of this world!

August 30th, they removed my subclavian, this good friend of mine… which had begun to malfunction… just 3 days before, they had to change it for the third time.

I now had to have an intravenous installed every couple of days!

A COMFORTING VISIT

August 21, 1979, I had a visit from David Jones, who had been one of the first patients to receive a bone marrow transplant for aplastic anemia in 1977 at the Princess Margaret Hospital. He had been a member of the Canadian Olympic canoeing team and was studying pre-medicine at Dalhousie University in Halifax.

His blood problem was the complete opposite of mine: instead of having too many immature white blood cells, he had less and less and his body therefore could not fight against infection. When he entered the hospital, he was so sick that he had nothing to lose: only an experimental bone marrow transplant could have saved his life.

He accepted to do it.

David had spent 85 days in isolation and, at the beginning, the graft did not take: the doctors were thinking of redoing the transplant, but finally the first white cells appeared. Then, he survived after a weight loss of nearly 70 pounds due to the chemotherapy, which was also making him nauseous.

It was after him that the medical staff learned to put patients on hyper-alimentation.

David, who was a star patient, had lots of people talking about him. He encouraged me a lot.

SCRABBLE® WITH A MASTER!

One day during my Toronto sojourn, I received a call from Lester Rubinovitch who was running my Montreal Scrabble® club in my absence.

He asked me if I would like to have someone with whom to play Scrabble® at the hospital. I told him what a pleasure it would be for me!

Not long after, I got a call from Mike Wise, who was director of the Toronto Scrabble® club!

Mike was a good guy, pleasant and friendly. He brought me biscuits that his wife Lynda had made.

He had the kindness of showing interest in playing with me, a stranger and one who was not as good a player as he.

I was very grateful.

Some hope on the horizon!
The next day Dr. Messner returned from his vacation and we spoke. He reassured me by telling me that the transplant seemed to be a success and if I couldn't walk yet, I would be able to soon enough. I could therefore return to Montreal. Not to my house of course, but to a rehab center.

As I was not recovering as quickly as he had predicted, Dr. Messner seemed to be of the opinion that the cause of my leg problems undoubtedly came from the Vincristine. He was thus confirming the opinion of the neurologist, Dr. Birnbaum: it was this chemotherapic medication which had damaged the nerves in my legs and caused my locomotion problem.

-I start physiotherapy
A physiotherapist from the Wellesley Hospital first came to work a bit with me by doing some leg stretches. It would take some time before the nerves could regenerate and my legs recover…

In the meantime, I had to have an EMG (electromyogram) to check the state of the nerves in my legs. For this test, I went to the Wellesley Hospital. It was at this hospital afterwards that I would get some physiotherapy.

Hope was on the horizon!

-A performing astronaut!
They put me in a kind of astronaut spacesuit intended to help me walk.

At least they were able to get me standing… so that I could move my legs vertically, as just about all the pressure was absorbed by the air of the spacesuit and not by my legs.

Four physiotherapists helped me stay erect in my spacesuit and walk through the parallel bars in front of me. Like that, I was able to do 2 or 3 laps in the bars. I was very excited!

Nevertheless, the exercise was not easy for me.

What a production I had to go through just to stand like a human!

-My family comes to celebrate Labour Day with me
On Labour Day I received a lot of visitors: my dad, my sisters, my brother, my cousin Louis from Chicago and 2 of my aunts and uncles from Montreal. It was a real family reunion.

-They take away the intravenous: I can take a bath!
On September 4th, they removed my intravenous, which meant that I could finally take a bath because I had no more tubes in me: I was very excited!

What a pleasure I had in the water that day: it was like a new birth. However, for the nurses who had to lift me out of my wheelchair to place me in the bathtub, it was not as exciting, but – as always, they did it in good spirits.

A new birth!

-They inform me of my return to Montreal!
Wednesday, September 12th, the nurses came in to tell me that I would be returning to Montreal in 2 days!

My mother had gone down to the cafeteria and so she didn't know the news yet.

When she returned to my room, I said to her… as a joke… that they had just informed me that I had to stay on for 2 more weeks. That meant that it would go beyond Rosh Hashannah (the Jewish New Year) and Yom Kippur (the Day of Atonement).

My mother was terribly disappointed because it was unthinkable for her to miss the high holidays. I caved in and told her that it was only a joke and that we would be returning "home in 2 days"!

My dear mother went from despair to jubilation: she had nevertheless accepted this big sacrifice… Dear mother!

-In Montreal, someone is thinking of me
For his part, Dr. Caplan was making the arrangements in Montreal to find a convalescent hospital where I would get the physiotherapy needed.

Hey! What happened to you?

SEPTEMBER 14, 1979, DEPARTURE FROM TORONTO

Finally, Friday September 14th arrived. I was returning to Montreal after 3 months in the hospital in Toronto. With emotion, I said good-bye to my doctors and to all my nurses at the Princess Margaret Hospital. Maureen, my favourite nurse, was not working that day and came specially to say farewell, wearing beautiful clothes instead of her uniform.

Ah! She was so charming! All these people who had worked for me would always remain in my heart. I would never forget their care, their physical and moral help and, above all, their kindness.
It was raining that day but it was so good to breathe in the outside air. It was great to see the city of Toronto which I hadn't seen since the month of June when I entered the hospital.
The ambulance came to get us, my mother and me, to drive us to the airport. I was transported on a stretcher.

-All aboard!
They first seated on the plane passengers with disabilities. They had reserved 2 seats just for me, so that they could lay my stretcher on them. When the regular passengers came aboard, one of them, an American, yelled out to me, "Hey! What happened to you?", and without waiting for an answer, continued down the aisle.

Evidently my response would have been very long! Where do I begin?

The flight only lasted an hour.

RECUPERATING AT THE JEWISH CONVALESCENT HOSPITAL OF LAVAL

Upon our arrival in Montreal, an ambulance was waiting for us as we got off the plane to drive us to the Jewish Convalescent Hospital of Laval. It is well-known for its good physiotherapy and occupational therapy programs.

As this hospital had no private rooms left, they put me into a semi-private room. My sister Gloria and her husband Gordon were already at the hospital to greet us. My father came and found us later.

Then Dr. Levin, the doctor assigned to me at this hospital, came to examine me.

-A well-organized hospital
The first day a dietician visited me. I listed the foods for her that I don't really like and those that I do like.

Fortunately, the food was kosher. For me that meant it was more familiar and tasty. It was a good thing since I would be staying 4½ months at this hospital!

I also met the physiotherapist Sheila Singer, who was adorable: we got along well together and laughed and laughed a lot. She was the sister of David Levine, a hospital administrator and – something that was very rare for a young Jew in 1979 – active member of the Parti Québecois.

The first 2 months at the Jewish Convalescent in Laval were rather calm.

-A military routine!

The daily program at this hospital as was presented to me:
- 07:45 a.m.: breakfast, Phew! Too early for me!
- After breakfast, an hour of physiotherapy:
- 11:30 a.m: lunch:
- 1:00 -2:00 p.m.: visiting hours:
- 4:30 p.m.: supper. Wow! For me, that's when I'd have a late lunch!
- at 5:30 p.m., everything was finished:
- from 7:00 – 9:00 p.m.: more visiting hours.

It was not easy for me to adjust to the schedule: me who gets up late, eats late and sleeps late!

-The visit of "my" Dr. Caplan
The first week, Dr. Stephen Caplan came to see me, anxious to see what transpired. I had the feeling that he considered me to be his "baby": it was thanks to him that I was able to have the transplant.

When the doctor was ready to leave, I asked him if I should worry about the radiation coming from the nearby television mounted on a stand at the end of my bed. The good doctor jokingly quipped, "No, if anything, after all the radiation you received, you'll give the t.v. radiation!".

-My nice week-end passes home
Fortunately, after the first 2 weeks spent at the Jewish Convalescent Hospital of Laval, you could go home for week-ends.

Something nice to look forward to! The first week-end that I spent at the house, all the neighbours came to see me and welcome me home. I couldn't wait until Friday night would come!

-Recurring Pneumonias
During this period, pneumonias made me go from one hospital to another. And so, in November 1979, 2 months after returning to Montreal, I was suffering from a bacterial pneumonia. I was sweating and went from shivering to a high temperature.

They transferred me to the Jewish General Hospital. They put in an i.v. – no doubt I was thrilled! My liver enzymes were elevated 8 times normal. I stayed at the Jewish General Hospital 2 weeks.

-My skin thins and becomes dry, tight and dark: hospitalization
At the end of November, I returned to the Jewish Convalescent in Laval, which was like my second home.

In mid-December, the same symptoms reappeared: another bacterial pneumonia, but this time it was more complicated. They returned me again to the Jewish General Hospital. I stayed there 5 long weeks. My liver enzymes were again elevated; my weight loss worsened and the skin on my limbs was becoming more and more thin, dry, tight and dark. The skin on my face took on a darkish colour… My visitors used to tell me that I had a nice tan. I didn't feel like laughing too much at the time: I wasn't in great shape. I was told much later on that they thought they might lose me.

-I improve bit by bit…
Slowly, my health began to improve, even if my weight did go from 160 to 120 lbs… Since I couldn't eat (no appetite and very dry mouth), I was fed by 2 tubes that went down my nose to my throat and to my stomach. A bit later on, I graduated to pureed food. I was nauseous just looking at a steak that was pureed!

Finally, I gained back some strength and returned to the convalescent hospital in Laval to get more physio.

Mid-January, 1980, I began to walk, with difficulty. Gradually, with diligent effort, I went from a wheelchair to a walker, from the walker to elbow crutches, from elbow crutches to 2 canes and then to one cane.

PERMANENT HOMECOMING AFTER 30 WEEKS IN HOSITALS

-Firstly, a sunny period!
At the beginning of February I finally was able to return home for good. I did, however, have to go to the Lethbridge Rehabilitation Center 3 times a week as an out-patient to continue with my physio and occupational therapy.

-I learn to walk again…
In the month of May, I went with my father to Beaver Lake.

At some point while walking, I just decided to abandon the cane and to walk without any support! A dream! It was as if, in an instant, I took back possession of my body. I felt so good about it! My health was improving gradually. I was able to walk, even if my balance weren't so good. But, at least, I was able to do so.

-Courses, work, a trip: an almost normal life!
I resumed my job as front desk clerk at the Holiday Inn La Seignurie in St. Laurent. I worked there part-time. I enjoyed this job a lot, except the fact that I had to be there at 7:00 am.: that was much too early for me…

In the spring of 1981, I was able to take a trip to Chicago and to Cincinnati for the Bat-Mitzvah of 2 of my cousins.

-A tour guide course
I really enjoyed the Montreal tour guide course: I learned a lot of interesting things about the city and its history. This course was twice a week at night; I was therefore still able to continue my work at the hotel.

-These activities interest me a lot, except that…
I really enjoyed all these activities, but I was having serious skin problems.

Since the transplant, in effect, the skin on my legs was gradually thinning and becoming very dry and quite tight.

It's easy to comprehend that blood has the greatest distance to travel to get to the legs, given how far they are from the heart.

THE DOCTORS TRY TO HEAL MY DRY, TIGHT SKIN ON MY LEGS

-I go to Toronto to consult with Dr. Messner
In November, 1981, Dr. Messner proposed my coming out to him in Toronto so he could see my legs and try to soothe my skin

problem. He would use a high dosage of Prednisone, a steroid, which given in large quantities could, according to him, relieve the tightness and fragility of my skin.

We went to Toronto, my mother and I, hoping this treatment would help.

-A very difficult period…
Too bad – this medication did not help me at all: after one month of use, I had horrible dreams and I became very impatient. My mother and I went for a few days to Toronto to see Dr. Messner at the Princess Margaret Hospital; it was I who drove!

After 5 weeks of this treatment on Prednisone, Dr. Messner decided to stop it, gradually reducing the dosage.

-A little ulcer that starts to climb and climb!
In December '81, a little ulcer appeared on my left foot. As a result, I had to interrupt the tourist guide course that I liked so much. On the recommendation of a friend, I went to consult a dermatologist in Laval. He prescribed to me Cothylène, a spray for open ulcers.

Unfortunately, not only did this medication not help me, but my ulcer deteriorated and the infection, going up my left leg, threatened to spread to my right leg. Dr. Caplan then referred me to Dr. Robin Billick, head of the department of dermatology at the Jewish General Hospital.

-After 3 months in the hospital, the ulcer invades both legs
Dr. Billick diagnosed severe pseudomonas, staphylococcus and candida infections; very wretched pathogenic bacteria responsible for skin infections.

In February 1982, Dr. Billick admitted me to the Jewish General Hospital where he treated me with antibiotics intravenously. He debrided my infected ulcers (that didn't tickle!), smeared Ihles

Paste (normally used for babies' behinds) and Flamazine (soothing cream for burns) and wrapped them up with bandages.

I spent 3 months in the hospital. Fortunately during this period I had a lot of visitors, relatives, friends and Scrabble® players.

-Returning home and again to the hospital.
Hardly a month after leaving the Jewish General Hospital, I had to return there with the same leg infections. Again I was treated with i.v. antibiotics for a month.

-The Doctors recommend I use a wheelchair!
This time in the hospital, however, the doctors watched me walking. My walking resembled that of a lame duck, since my balance wasn't great. I always chuckled to myself that I must have looked like a drunk and the joke was: I don't even drink!

The doctors recommended I use a wheelchair for a while to take the pressure off my legs and to avoid the stretching of the tight skin on my legs when I walk. They said to keep the legs elevated to increase blood circulation.

They obtained a wheelchair for me to use "for a while".

Adapting to the wheelchair in the house was not an easy task: we had to move around some furniture to make space. Moreover, as I didn't want to put aside my outside activities, I had to learn how to transport my wheelchair when I took the car.

My Aunt Evelyn, who suffered from Multiple Sclerosis which forced her to use a wheelchair for more than half her life, warned me: "You feel very comfortable in the chair, but be careful: you'll end up not wanting to leave it."

It was, in fact, very comfortable, in this "carriage", and I didn't feel like enduring the pains of walking.

A few months later, my doctors, noting that the use of the wheelchair had not helped the health of the skin on my legs, told me to stop using the chair and to start using my legs again.
--
-My dear Aunt had nevertheless warned me well
Alas, it was too late: my legs had lost too much strength… and the skin there had become tighter from the GVHD.

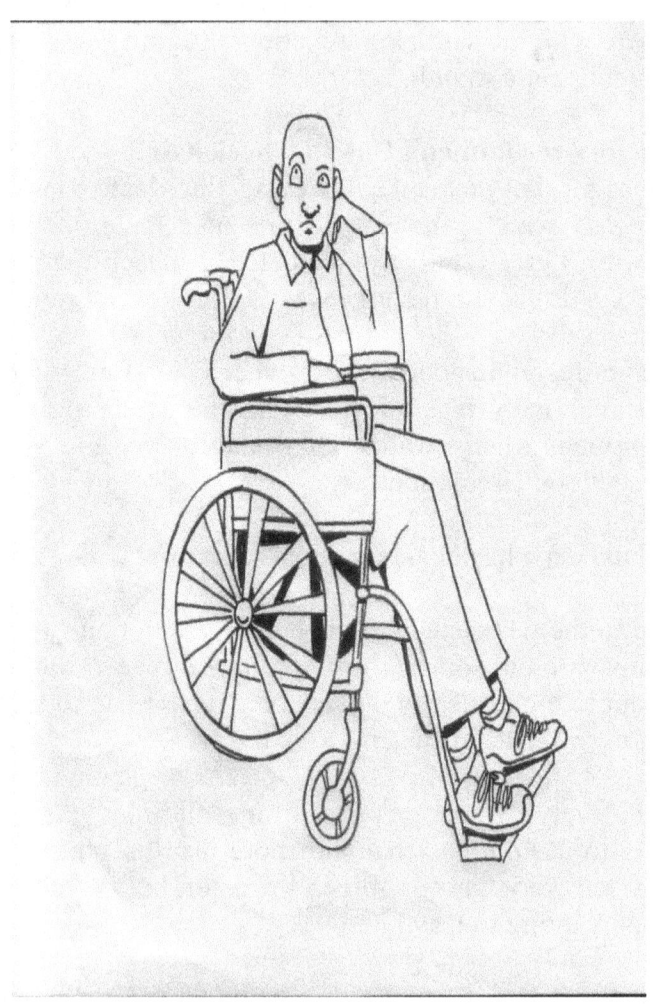

In effect, this carriage was very comfortable…

Dr. Billick, who was following me regularly, was worried about my legs. From the room next door to where I was sitting, he called Dr. Caplan. I heard him say, "Steve, his legs look terrible!". After his conversation, he came back to speak to me. And it was me who was trying to encourage him to not feel so bad!

-Another pseudomonas infection: another hospital stay
In October, '82, I had to spend another month at the Jewish General Hospital because of a new pseudomonas infection.

-I can always count on my parents
Thanks to the kindness of my parents, my homecomings – even if I took up a lot of space with my gear – were always pleasant.

Life was going along well enough for me, except that my body was suffering from a big dryness due to the radiation: my eyes (I must put eye drops in many times a day), my skin, my mouth… I couldn't eat like everybody. How my life would be so easy if I didn't have to eat! I always maintained that if I could take one pill for all 3 meals, I would save so much time!

Despite my problems and those that I imposed on my parents – life at home resembled a rather normal life.

My father rented, since I didn't have my own wheelchair to get around, a pretty heavy wheelchair to manipulate. He had to fold it and lift it into the trunk of the car, which demanded a lot from him. Nevertheless, despite his 61 years of age, he always did it without complaining. He encouraged me to go out with the family, my friends and to participate in my Scrabble club

-Another pneumonia: again a month in the hospital
At the beginning of February, 1983, I got pneumonia: I had to return to the Jewish General Hospital for a month of i.v. antibiotics.

Dr. Messner wants to attempt to save my legs!
In mid-January, 1984, Dr. Messner wanted to try to render the skin on my legs suppler and to heal my ulcers.

He requested I return to his hospital to treat me with Cyclosporin, an anti-rejection drug they now give to patients at the time of transplant to avoid the graft-versus-host disease.

-At the Princess Margaret Hospital, a treatment without effect
I went out to the hospital in Toronto. I stayed there 4 ½ months.
I had difficulty with the treatment: I developed some high blood pressure from the Cyclosporin and the skin on my legs broke down with infection. They put me on i.v. antibiotics: my legs improved; we gave Cyclosporin a second chance, but once again my legs broke down. Therefore, the treatment was completely stopped.
It was too late: Cyclosporin had to be administered at the time of the transplant.

A PATIENT WHO IS DIFFICULT TO FIND IN HIS HOSPITAL!

At the Princess Margaret Hospital in Toronto, I was in familiar country! I found friends.

One day, Anita Rackham, a good friend from my Montreal Scrabble club, was in Toronto on business and she wanted to visit me in the hospital. She called my room to speak to me. She asked my roommate, Maurice Delanoy from Saskatchewan, "Is Bernard there?" He answered her, not knowing where I was "I'm sorry… he's gone…"

All worried and upset, she asked, "What do you mean he's gone?" Realizing her angst, Maurice added, "Well he's gone out of the room to play Scrabble®! "

It could have happened that I was gone forever like some other patients. Fortunately, I was very much alive!

Also, Zev Kaufman, an expert Scrabble® player who was retired, had time to come play Scrabble® with me. We used to play in the hospital cafeteria until 1:00 in the morning!

One evening, the nurse who was in charge of treating my leg ulcers with mineral oil and then applying Flamazine cream, found me playing with Zev in the cafeteria. While smiling, she said to me, "When you have the time and you're not busy, call me and I'll come do your bandages!" I laughed: I was too busy for the nurses to do their work!

-Return home
In May, 1984, my cousin Hilda and her husband Jerry came from their visit in Chicago to visit me in the hospital in Toronto. I returned home to Montreal by car with them. With my parents at last!

-Another month-long stay in the hospital for pseudomonas...
In July, I had to return to the Jewish General Hospital to get i.v. antibiotics for pseudomonas again. Three months later (October 1984) I had to return for the same reason.

-Finished the comings and going to the hospital: I stay for 7 ½ months!
This time, Dr. Billick wanted to heal my leg ulcers once and for all by keeping me on bed rest with no pressure on my legs for as long as it took.

-At the end of 2 months, "permission"!
I nonetheless had the right to a week-end pass. I got permission to attend a Scrabble® tournament in Toronto.

At the end of the tournament, Sarah Pressman, who saw how unhappy I was to have to return to Montreal and to the hospital, said to me "So why don't you call in sick?!" I'm still laughing: a patient should call in to the hospital to say that they can't make it because they're sick!

-After the tournament, return to the hospital to finish my sentence!
To spend 7 1/2 months in the hospital could seem endless, but I adapted well: the washing, meals, phone calls, TV programs, visitors and above all, Scrabble®.

My hospital room was always busy. I used to play Scrabble often. I had the chance to play with someone from my Scrabble club, Linda Espallardo, a nurse in the coronary unit right near my room. She used to come in to play between her working hours.

There was also a good friend of the family, Celia Gordon, who would come to play a few games when she did volunteer work at the hospital.

-Hemangiomas which open just like that...
During this period, I developed eruptive hemangiomas: benign tumors on my legs that were made up of blood vessels which would open just like that, without provocation. It was peculiar: when the hemangioma erupted, a lot of pressure had to be put to stop the bleeding. Only Dr. Billick was able to permanently get rid of them: he would freeze the hemangioma, remove it and then cauterize it. He even published an article on this phenomenon in the prestigious New England Journal of Medicine.

Once a hemangioma began to bleed incessantly onto my hospital room floor and I rang for the nurse to come quickly. Of course no one answered and after a few minutes. I decided that something had to be done, so I used my phone to call the hospital, I asked to be connected to the 2NE nursing station (literally right across the hall from my room) and when someone soon answered the phone, I said who I was and that I was bleeding nicely onto the floor- THEN, I got a nurse to come in!

A Banal... Acute Pericarditis!
One day in the spring of 1985, I was suffering from abdominal pains so acute that I couldn't stop complaining. Dr. Caplan

requested Dr. Spanier come see me, "An excellent surgeon", he assured me.

I will never forget what the surgeon uttered to me while laughing from the door to my room. "Would you feel better the way you are or if I cut you up?" I answered him in pain and unable to control my laughter, "Doctor, don't make me laugh: it hurts too much!"

It was later discovered that I had pericarditis, an inflammation around the heart, which went away by itself not long afterwards.

-My 7 ½ month internment comes to an end!
Realizing the little progress achieved during this long hospitalization, Dr. Billick decided that my hospital stay had gone on long enough. He concluded that, despite all the care I received, my legs would never heal and that he was going to treat me as an external patient any time my legs would flare up. He said to me, "Go out! Have fun! Get on with your life!

We will do whatever's possible according to the situation."

Over the years, I tried numerous medications. Most would work for a while but then it would be necessary to replace it for another one whose effect was just as temporary… All the skin problems were still a manifestation of the graft-versus-host disease.

Afterwards, I often had to be on oral antibiotics because of chronic leg ulcer infections. The skin was thin, dry, tight and discolored.

It was a chronic battle: I would go on antibiotics and the leg ulcers would improve a bit: the moment I went off the antibiotics, the infection would come back.

MY FRIENDS, THE NURSES

When you're hospitalized for a long time, you become "institutionalized': the days and weeks go by very quickly. The people with whom you're always in contact are obviously the nurses:

-Miss Goldfinger was the head nurse of 2 Northeast internal medicine. I called her "Silver Toes" (the opposite of Goldfinger), but never to her face. She ran a tight ship, exacting from the nurses as much as she exacted from herself: she made it her duty – one would even say her pleasure – to know the names of all the patients on the floor. Everyone, including the doctors, respected her. Shirley, a Jamaican nurse, loved to laugh with her good friend Fanor, a Chinese nurse. Both would come to my room to chat. As for Pat Beck, she used to have deep discussions with me and we couldn't stop ourselves from laughing! Manon Bellehumeur, who lived up to her name "Good Humour", was very sympathetic and always had a warm smile. I loved to tease her. Helen, the Greek nurse always liked to laugh so much.

-Réjeanne, an older nurse: she was very funny with her sarcastic tone! And finally, Miss Ford from the Caribbean, who was very serious and formal, but I learned how to make her smile.

All the nurses liked me and spoiled me.

RETURN HOME TO "GET ON WITH MY LIFE"!

-Installation at the house: some things adapted to my physical condition
In the spring of '86, I was able to buy myself a light wheelchair and had elevated leg pieces made especially for it (I always had to keep my legs elevated for better blood circulation).

Moreover, the Handicapped Persons Bureau of Quebec paid for the purchase of an exterior elevator platform on the balcony as well as for the necessary work for its installation. We had to get rid of half the garden to place it there.

Various people contributed to the installation of this hydraulic lift: even our neighbours – whose house is attached to ours – contributed by willingly accepting this exterior device which, not being the most elegant, could depreciate their property.

Thanks to this elevator, I could have access from the exterior to the front door. I was therefore free to come in and go in my wheelchair: I was independent. My father gave me his car whenever I wanted. I was able to put my wheelchair into the trunk myself and then get into the driver's seat.

-I take advantage of my independence: I organize my life
At home, I began doing more tutoring. It was the time when English-speaking nurses began having to pass a French proficiency exam.

This was more than just a rewarding experience for me; I was able to put a bit of money aside.

-At the age of 27, I get the shingles!
At the end of spring, 1986, I contracted the shingles on the right side of my face. A childhood disease (chicken pox), I once again had to be hospitalized for 2 weeks! As I suffered with terrible pains at times on the face, I took advantage of the situation to give myself a new look: I grew a little beard, a fantasy which made my visitors laugh!

-And life goes on!
In the summer of 1986, I went to Vancouver with my cousin Minda to visit Expo '86.

I also returned to UQAM to continue my courses in Tourism Management part-time, very part-time!

-Life! Life!
During a surprise party for my 30th birthday July 25th, 1988, one of my friends, Ron Sigal, told me that he was leaving soon on a trip to California. I asked him, just like that, if I could accompany him.

Even though it was really last-minute – and to go with a person in a wheelchair was a real adventure – he accepted! We had a great trip!

-I am offered to teach for a few hours
In autumn, 1986, I was offered to teach "games" 3 hours per week as part of a new program at an elementary school. I enjoyed the position.

-A nice trip to London!
In 1990, I also had a golden opportunity to go to England and Scotland again with Ron for 2 weeks. We visited London and its surroundings and drove all the way up to Edinburgh (I really enjoyed driving on the left-hand side).

-I succeed in getting my Bachelor's "while I'm alive": to be celebrated!
In 1994 I finally received … while still being alive … my Bachelor's degree in Tourism Management! In October, I organized a big graduation party: I had always maintained that if I were still alive when I graduated, I would make myself a big party to celebrate! That's what I did! I invited all those whom I liked.

I was very happily surprised to see Lynda and Mike Wise who came in specially from Toronto. I was extremely happy and moved to receive Dr. Caplan and his wife. My childhood and Scrabble® friends were there as was my whole, big family.

Mike gave a speech as funny as it was moving. My friend Fran spoke and my nephew Richard sang. As for me, I read a poem I had composed for the occasion.

-"Just For Laughs" … but not so funny!
In 1998, during the week preceding my 40th birthday, I was feeling chest pains.

Despite these pains, believing they were some kind of indigestion, I went to the "Just For Laughs" Festival with my good friend

Debbie. During that evening I had a bad pain in my chest and I found it somewhat hard to breathe!

-An acute heart attack!
Since I didn't have a general practitioner following the transplant, I consulted Dr. Caplan who had me do an electro-cardiogram.

When he got the results the next day, he had me return for a more precise cardiac test. Once the test was over, I began getting dressed when the cardiologist asked me, "Where are you going?" Surprised by his question, I answered him that I was going home. He retorted, "You're going nowhere! You just had an acute MI (myocardial infarction)!"

Upon hearing this, I almost had a heart attack! (ha! ha!) I couldn't understand how someone like me could have a heart attack: I was young, thin and I wasn't stressed.

The cause was undoubtedly from the excessive amount of radiation I had received at the time of the transplant (500 rads for 5 minutes to each side of my body). All this manifested itself 19 years later! The doctors know today not to give so much radiation all at once.

-And here I am in the Coronary Care unit!
Following this heart attack, they put me in the CCU (Coronary Care Unit): I couldn't believe that they had brought me there! They hooked me up to a machine that monitored my heartbeats, my pulse and my oxygen level.

-I narrowly avoid an invasive heart procedure
The doctors were talking about doing an angiogram on me (it assesses heart damage and if need be, opens up blocked arteries), but I really feared this invasion of a catheter towards the heart... I said to myself that with all my problems, if they opened up a little area in the skin to filter through the catheter, my fragile skin may not heal there.

At any rate, my cardiologist decided not to go ahead with the angiogram. He opted for a few nuclear medicine tests which determined the amount of damage to my heart.

It appeared that the heart attack damaged 25% of my heart.

The cardiologist was of the opinion that I could live like that, without performing an angiogram, and I would take medications for the heart and blood pressure. He felt I was young enough and would be okay.

-A disappointment
During the hospital stay, I had to unfortunately cancel my participation in the National Scrabble® Championship in August, 1998 in Chicago.

A representative from the Scrabble® Company called to ask me how I was doing. He told me he was going to send me some souvenirs from this tournament in which all the good players were participating. I was very touched by their concern and honour they gave me.

…And a big loss
Another phone call, sad and touching, was the one announcing the passing of my good friend Mike Wise, who was always interested in me and my family. My mother, who feared that this news would affect me greatly after my heart attack, had tried to not reveal it to me. I knew that Mike had a lot of health problems, but never did I think that he could die … Ironically, it was also at the Princess Margaret Hospital that he spent the last days of his life.

-They send me home with a strict diet!
I was next referred to a dietician. This, I wasn't expecting! Me, who detests so much the chore of eating and not liking so many foods, here now they're going to impose on me the why and wherefore!

Up until then, since I was very thin, I was told to eat caloric foods like milkshakes and cakes. Now, everything I like was no longer permitted: smoked meat sandwiches, hamburgers, pizzas, cakes, pies, chocolates, cookies and salted nuts.

I was devastated: everything that tastes good, I could no longer eat!

-...A diet which didn't please my folks either
My mother wasn't happy either with this diet which made her buy me things that she had never bought before, like natural peanut butter (almost in a liquid form), natural yogurt instead of ice cream, etc. When she felt too frustrated, she told me to go buy those things myself.

My father wasn't too happy either. He used to say to me "Well, this won't kill you: it's good. eat it!"

-In the long run ...
I must admit that, with time and on occasions, I began to cheat and today I eat a lot of things I'm not allowed (I'm only fooling myself!). I nonetheless maintained the essential parts of this diet: whole wheat bread, 1% milk, no fried foods, salmon twice a week – even though I don't like fish – I eat it because I know it's good for me.

VISIT TO THE PRINCESS MARGARET HOSPITAL

In 1998, while in Toronto for a Scrabble® tournament, I couldn't resist the desire to make a pilgrimage to the Princess Margaret Hospital. I was able to verify the progress they had made medically thanks to medical research over 20 years. When I received my transplant in 1979, they were doing one transplant at a time; now, they do 3 at a time! They were coming from all over Canada. I was proud of the progress of medical research: after all, I had participated in it… in a certain way!

-News… from transplants back then

Alas, news from those who had gone through transplants at the same time as I, that is to say from 1979 onward, was not all rosy either:

-Back In 1984 yet, my roommate Maurice Delanoy from Saskatchewan, had died. He was a soft-spoken newlywed who worked for Saskatchewan Hydro. The skin on his face turned very dark as a result of the GVHD. He suffered a massive brain hemorrhage one morning.

-Some others died, including a young lady from Alberta who passed away when she returned home…

-From Edmonton, a teenager had suffered the same fate…

-And David Jones from Nova Scotia, the idol of the nurses, a handsome funny guy, a sportsman and an athlete who was preparing to become a doctor, had died of anemophily, which is lack of white blood cells.

Me, I was a survivor… I could have easily had the same fate as them. I still remember that time when I had gone out of our room; Maurice Delanoy had answered my friend Anita's question on the phone by saying, "He's gone." When he heard Anita get all frantic, he continued, "He's gone out of the room!"

This could have happened that I was gone for good, me too … Fortunately for me, I was very much alive.

A MENINGIOMA! WILL IT BE NECESSARY TO OPEN UP THE SKULL?

During the summer of 2000, I began to get very bad headaches. I went to finally check them out at the emergency of the Jewish General Hospital where they discovered a meningioma in the brain, a kind of benign tumor which develops in the meninges, the arachnoids and the pia matter.

-The brain tumor threatens my left eye…
This little non-cancerous tumor was blocking my right optic nerve and was eventually going to cover my left optic nerve if we didn't "see" to it.

They took me on a stretcher into one of the emergency department's rooms to wait for Dr. Jeffrey Minuk, a neurologist. I was very worried.

I began thinking of my Aunt Gladys, my father's sister, who unfortunately had to have her skull opened so that the doctors could determine to what extent her brain cancer had spread… They closed it up almost immediately because they saw that they couldn't do anything for her. After this operation she was never the same: she had difficulty finding her words and she became very emotional.

The doctor kept me in the hospital for a few days to examine me and he told me that the final decision as to what to do would be up to the chief neurosurgeon, Dr. Gerard Mohr. Since he was away for 2 months, Dr. Minuk released me from the hospital awaiting his return.

-At the time of my transplant, they had warned me of the effects of Prednisone …
Ten years earlier, in 1990, the vision in my right eye was beginning to deteriorate. My ophthalmologist at the Jewish General Hospital, Dr. Rosen, was waiting for my cataract in the right eye to develop large enough before removing it. At the time of my transplant, they had warned me that I could develop cataracts because of the steroid Prednisone.

They hospitalize me in order to remove the cataract…
December 8, 1992, the time had come to remove this cataract. I couldn't wait to see clearly again (my field of vision in that right

eye was becoming more and more limited). However, since I was not your normal patient because of the transplant, Dr. Rosen decided – where normally such an operation is done in 4 hours as an outpatient – to admit me to the hospital for a few days.

... But they release me right away without operating!
The doctors from the ophthalmology department all consulted on my case and the decision was taken to send me home without operating. It would serve no purpose to remove the cataract since there was damage to the right optic nerve.

I was thus referred to a neuro-ophthalmologist, Dr. Ganz. He was intrigued by the fact that the optic nerve was affected in only one eye. I asked him if the Vincristine which had caused my peripheral neuropathy in my legs in August, 1979, could be the cause. This was not his opinion (now, the meningioma that had just been discovered in July, 2000, explained the gradual loss of vision in my right eye).

-My sister Gloria finds an alternative to surgery!
In the meantime, my sister Gloria – who has been my guardian angel since the beginning – spoke to one of her friends whose son had suffered from a brain tumor.

They had gone to Providence, Rhode Island, to consult with Dr. Jorg Noren, a celebrated neurosurgeon who specialized in a type of radiosurgery called Gamma Knife, a non-invasive procedure.

-The famous Gamma Knife
The Gamma Knife consists of high frequency electromagnetic waves which bombard the skull from the exterior, without having to open it.

It is made up of ionizing rays which can destroy, with precision, the tumour without touching the rest of the brain. No conventional surgery is necessary and the patient can return home after the treatment.

-In the summer of 2000, I go to Rhode Island to consult with the specialist
Since, in August, 2000, I had a North American Scrabble® tournament which happened to be taking place in Providence, Gloria's friend suggested that I go meet Dr. Noren. Normally, I had to wait for the return of Dr. Mohr at the Jewish General Hospital to know what to do in my case.

Nevertheless, I absolutely wanted to find an alternative to an operation on the skull. I decided to go and consult with this specialist.

-A "real" specialist!
I was amazed to see a celebrated brain surgeon sit down with the eventual patient that I was, to discuss my case for 3 hours. I felt total confidence in him.

According to him, it was possible for me to be a candidate for Gamma Knife radiosurgery. However, before confirming this, he wanted me to take a more precise MRI (Magnetic Resonance Imaging).

I then took the MRI back in Montreal and Dr. Noren, after analyzing it, accepted me as a patient for Gamma Knife.

-A procedure... not paid for by RAMQ (Régie de L'Assurance Maladie du Québec)
In September, 2000, when Dr. Mohr finally returned to Montreal, I went with my parents to consult with him and speak to him about my visit to Rhode Island.

-Dr. Mohr approves the Gamma Knife in my case
First of all, Dr. Mohr told me that a conventional brain operation to remove the tumor was out of the question. He was in favour of Gamma Knife, considering all that I had undergone since the transplant.

-A very expensive procedure
However, he underlined that this type of intervention was not covered by RAMQ (the cost was $23,000 U.S.). RAMQ promoted what was available in Quebec- the LINAC approach (Linear Accelerated Radiography) which also sends electronic particles in the brain to irradiate the lesions.

-Dr. Noren is of the same opinion
Dr. Noren maintained that LINAC was not as precise as Gamma Knife: there was a risk, according to him, of irradiating the area around the tumor.

It was therefore necessary to begin steps to go after RAMQ to assume the cost of the Gamma Knife treatment.

-Eventual legal proceedings against RAMQ?
According to Dr. Mohr, it would always be possible if ever RAMQ absolutely refused to reimburse the costs for the necessary treatment, to sue them. However, those who tried to do it before had always failed.

Dr. Mohr recommended pursuing my treatment with Dr. Noren since Gamma Knife wasn't yet available in Canada and I had already started with him.

-RAMQ does not agree!
Upon approaching RAMQ to pay for my treatment, they demanded that I consult their doctor, Dr. Bahary, a radiology specialist at the Notre Dame Hospital. He told me that he had worked with Gamma Knife in the United States.

According to him, it would be too dangerous for me: if it missed its target, it could cause irreparable damages. Accordingly, he said he was going to recommend to the government to reject my request.

I decided just the same to pursue my steps towards Gamma Knife. I made an appointment at the Rhode Island Hospital in Providence. The procedure was set for December 18, 2000.

-Lawyer Harvey Lazare's precious help
Fortunately, I had the help of my good friend Debbie's husband, Harvey Lazare, who was a lawyer. A precious help.

Harvey maintained that the law stipulated that "If 2 specialists say that a patient needs to receive a treatment that is not available in Quebec, the Régie de l'assurance Maladie du Québec must pay for it at the place where it is available".

What's more, Harvey knew that he could count on the 2 specialists (neurosurgeons) at the Jewish General Hospital – Drs. Mohr and Berger. He was convinced that with time and a lot of patience, the steps taken against RAMQ could succeed in making them reimburse for the treatment.

-Gamma Knife Intervention
On December 17, 2000, my parents drove me to the Rhode Island Hospital where they initially gave me valium. I had never been so relaxed in my life!

They screwed on a large apparatus to my head and then took an MRI in order to verify that it was properly placed.

The technicians then proceeded to attach a helmet to the apparatus and to make the precise calculations for the Gamma Knife's direction. They had me enter a machine a few times, where I was exposed to a couple of minutes of Gamma rays. They adjusted the helmet each time I entered. The treatment lasted 20 minutes.

The Meningioma Is Bombarded!
The meningioma, the whole meningioma and nothing but the meningioma was thus bombarded. The hope was that the Gamma Knife would change the DNA of the meningioma so that it would cease progressing and would diminish with time.

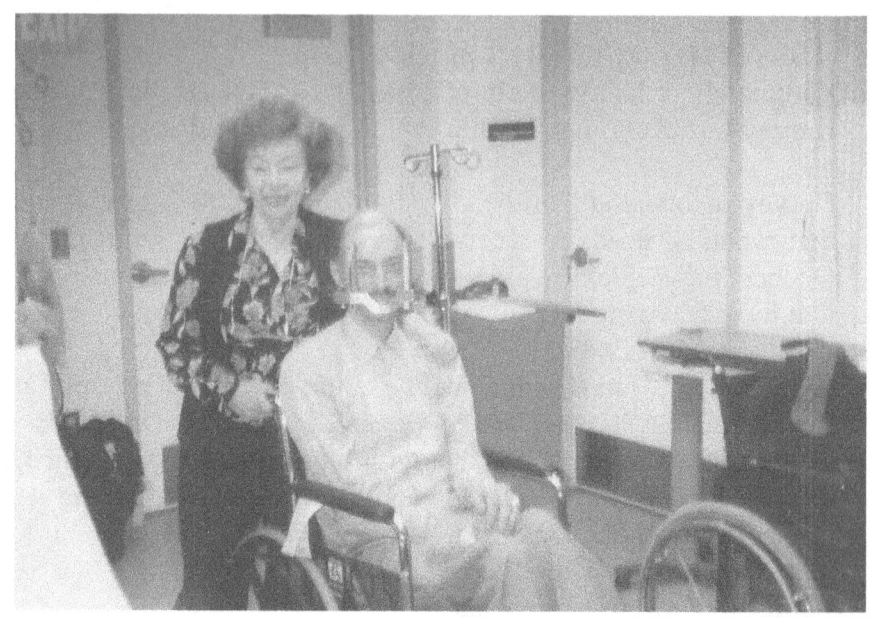

My mother and I after they attached the apparatus for Gamma Knife

-The procedure is a success … with a hitch

Once done, they removed the helmet and apparatus. I never felt anything at all! They kept me just the same overnight in the hospital.

However, Dr. Noren had to inform me that to reach the left optic nerve to save it from the meningioma, he unfortunately had to pass through the right optic nerve (thus damaging it more)…

In so doing, from my right eye where my visual perception was just about nil, I can no longer even distinguish any light at all from complete darkness.

I was just as happy to have been able to avoid the worst.

SUCCESS IN PURSUING RAMQ!

In the meantime, Harvey was pursuing his case against RAMQ.

Since we were suing RAMQ, we had to go before the TAQ (Tribunal Administratif du Québec), which had 2 judges: one a lawyer, the other a doctor. Never before had a case suing RAMQ for access to Gamma Knife been pushed so far.
Certainly RAMQ tried to confound Dr. Noren, one of the pioneers of Gamma Knife in Sweden. This big specialist believed so much in his cause that he flew up specially from Rhode Island at his own expense to appear before the TAQ.

This brain surgeon did not even charge for his time!

BRAVO! HARVEY BEARS FRUIT FOR HIS EFFORTS!

Finally after one year, in 2004, both judges sided with us. They supported Harvey's argument: "If 2 specialists recommend a treatment which is not available in Quebec, RAMQ must pay for it."

Both judges were of the opinion that Gamma Knife was the most appropriate choice in my case due to the risks of the inaccuracy of LINAC, which even more so, has to be applied a few times. With Gamma Knife, the procedure is done all at once. RAMQ was therefore obliged to reimburse the $23,000 cost.

-A victory for all of Quebec!
I could never have imagined that we could win against the government.

It was a victory from which all Quebecers could profit.
Bravo Harvey, and thank you!
And thank you, Dr. Noren!

2002-2003: THE HOUSE…THE HOSPITALS…THE HOUSE…

-Trips with my friends
Over the summers of 2002 and 2003, I had the pleasure and opportunity to travel by car across the United States with some Scrabble® players. We did not have a lot of time to visit the tourist sites that we would have liked to have known, but we were able to admire the beautiful scenery, the Rocky Mountains and then spend some time in Las Vegas.

-However, my leg ulcers worsen…
In October, 2004, Dr. Joseph Portnoy, head of infectious diseases at the Jewish General Hospital, put me on i.v. antibiotics to treat the ulcer infections that had developed on my legs: pseudomonas again. Only this time, I was put on a PICC line (Peripherally Inserted Central Catheter) which is inserted into the upper arm in a procedure done in radiology. The PICC line allows you to avoid hospitalization.

-They show me how to give myself antibiotics at home
The nurses from the CLSC (Local Community Service Center), who were coming daily to my house to do my dressing on my legs, showed me how to give myself the antibiotics. The nurse would have to change the connections twice a week.

The inconvenience for me was that my i.v. wires were hooked up to a little purse containing the PICC line's pump, which I had to take everywhere I went. At least I was able to attend to my normal activities: teaching chess, going to my Scrabble® club and playing poker.

"I'm sorry Bernard. I'm sorry…"

-The PICC line lets me go out. Yes, but…
One week after they put in the PICC line, I decided – despite my father's objections – to go to my friend Bruce's for our weekly poker game.

Since having the intravenous, I found it cumbersome to bum down his stairs to the basement. I asked my friend Murray, a very strong guy, to carry me down where we were playing. He lifted me up easily from my wheelchair, but he stumbled over a first step before the basement stairs and we both went flying down the 5 stairs…

Poor Murray! I could still hear him repeating, while trying to wipe away some blood that was coming from his nose: "I'm sorry Bernard. I'm sorry."

As for me, when I tried to move, I felt a sharp pain in my right hip. I was hoping that the pain would subside so that I could join the group that was waiting for me.

In the meantime, my friends were wondering what they should do for me: the last thing I wanted was to call my father! They decided there was no alternative but to call an ambulance, then… they called my father just the same.

-The paramedics arrive
Fifteen minutes later, an Urgence Santé ambulance arrived. However, the paramedics couldn't put me on a stretcher because the angle of the basement door denied the stretcher access. Four of them held me up like a board: one on each side of my body, one in back to support my head and one in front to support my legs. If you heard loud screaming that night, it was me! (I would not have wanted my father to see me in that state!)

Once in the ambulance, they placed me on a stretcher.

-I break my right hip…
They drove me to the hospital, trying to drive slowly over bumps to avoid further discomfort. I spent 6 weeks in the hospital.

-… And I have water on my lungs...
As I was feeling a bit feverish and had some difficulty breathing, the doctors had to first take care of the water on my lungs that developed after the fall I had. They gave me oxygen: it was scary for a while as my breathing became more laborious. The scariest thing is when you don't know where your next breath is coming from! They had to still operate on my hip.

-And, featuring, "C Difficile!"
Nevertheless, the night before my operation, a doctor came into my room to inform me that I had caught Clostridium Difficile, a bacteria which causes diarrhea and other more serious intestinal diseases like colitis: it was everywhere in the hospitals.

-They have to operate on my hip, even though I have "C Difficle"!
The doctors decided to operate on me just the same. On November 12th, 2004, after giving me an epidural, the doctors installed a metal plate into the right hip. They then placed me into a room with another patient who also had C Difficile.

-A necessary post-operative physiotherapy
Certainly a few days after such an operation, I had to receive some physiotherapy…

But, since C Difficile was raging throughout the entire Jewish General Hospital, no internal patient was allowed into the physio department. The Clostridium Difficile epidemic was also rampant in all the hospitals: hospital services, like physiotherapy were closed to internal patients, many of whom were contaminated. Only external patients could receive physio.

They therefore sent me home so that I could come to the clinic as an external patient.

-…As an external patient… and … in winter!
What they were asking me to do was extremely difficult for me in my state… especially because it was winter.

-It's a retired physiotherapist who comes to my rescue!
My cousin Mindy, who is a physiotherapist, initially came to my house to give me some treatments.

Following that, Ellie Rubin, a recently retired physiotherapist who knew me, offered to come give me the necessary care. She came to my house voluntarily to treat me twice a week for several months. I was so lucky!

I had a lot of gratitude for this exceptional woman. Thanks to her, I was able to find some autonomy again.

In March, 2005, pseudomonas came back again. Dr Portnoy put me back on the PICC line to treat the leg infections.

I went regularly to his infectious disease clinic while still being followed by Dr. Billick and now someone else, Lincoln D'Souza. A woman who was a representative for Smyth & Nephew Pharmaceutical had recommended the latter, who was a specialist clinician nurse at the Royal Victoria Hospital Wound Care Clinic.

I wanted to go down from the sidewalk to the road

-Again another accident!
In November, 2005, I was coming out of the dentist's office to get into an adapted transport vehicle. I wanted to descend backwards from the sidewalk onto the road and had asked the driver to hold my wheelchair while so doing. Thinking that she was there, I toppled over backwards and fell onto the street hitting the back of my head!

As for the woman who was the adapted transport driver, she didn't even wait until the ambulance arrived. She even left with my bag that she initially took from me and had placed into the trunk!
It was an adapted transport inspector who, having to make out an incident report, brought me back my bag and admitted to me that the driver was wrong to have left me like that.

-Six stitches to the head...
At the Jewish General Hospital emergency, still from being in wet pants when I landed on the snow on the road, they gave me 6 stitches to the head and then I returned home...

The next day, I had the chills and I feared having to be rehospitalized. The following day, I nonetheless went for my appointment at the Royal Victoria Hospital to see Lincoln for him to do my leg bandages.

-...And 2 weeks in the hospital!
Unfortunately, I was shivering so much that Lincoln sent me to the emergency department.

The next day they transferred me to the Jewish General Hospital because all my doctors and records are there.

They treated me for a possible diverticulitis with antibiotics intravenously for 2 weeks.

OCTOBER, 2006, PREPARATION BEGINS FOR ... AN AMPUTATION

Time was moving on and my leg ulcers were not healing.

One day, Dr. Portnoy asked me while looking at a big, ugly ulcer on my right foot, "You like this? You need this? You know that there is an alternative?" I knew right away what he meant and I answered him, "And who says my skin would heal after this... alternative?" "Yes," he responded, "You are definitely right. But know that there is an alternative just the same."

I was put back on the PICC line August 29th, 2006 at the Royal Victoria Hospital. Dr. Billick used liquid nitrogen to burn off the excessive skin which was forming around the ugly-looking ulcer on the right ankle, hoping to stop the bleeding...

What's more is that Lincoln decided, from his standpoint, to take a little biopsy of this terrible ulcer to ascertain why there wasn't any improvement. A few weeks later, he made an appointment with a plastic surgeon, Dr. Harvey Brown, at the Royal Victoria Hospital.

-Then... the naked truth: "We have to cut!"
When Dr. Brown saw the ulcer and learned of the biopsy results, he said, "I'm afraid it's necessary to cut the leg from the knee down... you have skin cancer." (squamous-cell carcinoma).

Immediately the famous words of Dr. Portnoy came back to me. The moment I was dreading so much had arrived...

I thought I was having a bad dream.

I asked Dr. Brown if there was an alternative to an amputation. The good doctor answered me, "If there was a plastic microsurgeon who would be able to excise the cancer and recover the area left open with a small piece of skin which could be stretched, perhaps we could consider it..." He then made an appointment for me with Dr. Lessard who had a reputation for doing miracles.

-A jovial intern comes to console me...
After Dr. Brown left, an intern came in to explain my cancer to me, "There are 3 kinds of skin cancer:

> 1- basal cell, which grows on the skin surface and could easily be removed:
> 2- squamous cell, which is found just underneath the skin and could be excised without too much difficulty;
> 3- melanoma – the worst skin cancer which is deeper in the skin and can be deadly; it can develop rapidly and be very aggressive."

Then the intern jovially informed me that I had, "the second best skin cancer!"

-Phew! I'm so lucky!
"But, in your case" added the intern – undoubtedly to mitigate the good news – "it would not be possible to excise the cancer and keep the ankle, because you do not have healthy skin to graft over the hole left by the excision."

My skin was, in effect, always dry like silk paper, thin, tight and sclerotic... But how could I function... without my leg?

-Things are going too fast!
I was astounded by all this information: how could I lose a part of me?

-Searching for contrary opinions
I then started to ask the opinion of several people:

- that of Dr. Billick:

- that of Allen, a cousin who is a plastic surgeon:

- that of my friend Ellie, the physiotherapist, who was always after me to have this amputation done. According to her, I would get rid of an enormous problem and, in so doing: the rest of my strength could concentrate on other problems...

All those to whom I turned were of the same opinion: I should undergo the amputation.

When I finally met with Dr. Lessard, she immediately said after looking at my ulcer, "I would like you to be seen by Dr. Michel Turcotte at the Montreal General Hospital: he is head of the oncology and orthopedic surgery department."

I knew right away that she made up her mind that she couldn't do anything. She would leave the responsibility of giving me the bad news to Dr. Turcotte.

-A decisive meeting
Not long after, I met Dr. Turcotte.

When he saw my leg, he shook his head. I knew instantly that he was going to reject the idea of a simple graft and opt for amputation...

According to him, in effect, there was no other choice. He convinced me to accept it. I liked this doctor. I had a lot of confidence in him. I gave in to his judgment.

-A doctor like a psychologist
To help me along the way, he sent me to see Dr. Denis Duranleau at the Montreal Rehabilitation Institute to see what kind of prosthesis they could put on after the amputation.

My visit to Dr. Duranleau defined my situation. He imagined a kind of artificial leg in which I would put my stump... I would thus be able to walk a little bit using a walker.
Little by little, I was accepting the idea.

OCTOBER 31, 2006: AMPUTATION OF MY RIGHT LEG

The operation was done at the Montreal General Hospital.
The morning of October 31st, I had to be there for 6:00 a.m.
Unimaginable for me: it was still night time!
Towards what nightmare… was I going?
....
They gave me an epidural instead of a general anesthetic.
Without a doubt, thanks to that epidural, I fell asleep during the amputation.

During the operation, they installed a device at the base of my spine which emitted pain medication at regular intervals.

When I woke up an hour later, I was in the recovery room.

Obviously, my first act was to see what was left of my leg: I was comforted all the same to find out that Dr. Turcotte had left my knee cap… I must also say that I didn't feel, to my great surprise, any major pains nor above all the phantom pain that many amputees feel after losing a limb.

The Period of Adjustment:

-Post operation at the Montreal General Hospital
I stayed three weeks at the Montreal General Hospital. In one way, I was fortunate: at this hospital, you ordered what you wanted at each meal and then room service would deliver it. I had never been so spoiled!

To my great relief, within a few days I was already able to transfer into my wheelchair on one leg.

-The Catherine Booth Convalescent Hospital
-I was then transferred to the Catherine Booth Convalescent Hospital to receive physiotherapy treatment. I remained there for four weeks during which I was allowed to go out on passes, like going to my Scrabble® club with my friends.

-The Montreal Rehabilitation Institute

In mid-December, 2006, the stump was fully healed and ready to fit into a prosthesis. I was admitted to the Montreal Rehabilitation Institute where I could go home on week-ends. I received excellent physio and occupational therapies.

However, as I hadn't really walked in years, it was very difficult to do so even with the prosthesis. When I tried to walk, I instinctively walked on my tippy-toes because of contractures and my tight, tight skin which always risked ulcerating – and my head was down towards my shoulders. The specialists understood that I could not walk long distances with my prosthesis: it would only serve me for going up stairs and doing some exercises… After four and a half months at this institute, they discharged me to go home. I had to go on the PICC line again for three months, from September to December, 2007.

DECEMBER 12, 2008: THE MOST PAINFUL MOURNING

THE PASSING OF MY MOTHER WHOM I LOVED SO MUCH…

My mother died this day, and I am devastated.

She was my whole world.

I lost there, really, the most important part of my body, and my best friend.

My mother was sweet and serene.

Even though it wasn't easy having a son like me, her courage helped me through all the bad stages of my life!

She suffered the physical pains just as much as I did.

I could always count on her and her calming presence. She was especially there at the time of the transplant, all my setbacks and hospitalizations.

We loved each other very much: she used to say to me how good I was whereas I used to tell her that she was better.

It was a big loss for me.

I do not think she's really gone.

MY DEAR LEFT LEG

After the amputation of my right leg in 2006, the ulcers on my left leg and foot continued to deteriorate.

This leg made me suffer a lot. A lot more than the right one had ever done.

Nurses were coming to the house almost every day to treat my purulent ulcers and redo my bandages.

In November, 2009 after taking a few biopsies, Dr. Billick called me at home (he was now more vigilant in keeping any eye on my developing ulcers since my amputation in 2006). I wasn't shocked to hear his verdict: I had almost expected it. He was recommending amputation of my left leg since it too was found to have the same cancer as the other one had. To soften his verdict a little, he assured me that it would be possible to keep the knee cap as they did with my right leg.

Certainly, the decision was still very difficult. I dreaded a second amputation. The idea to no longer have contact with the ground frightened me…

I therefore went back to see Dr. Turcotte, the doctor who had performed the first amputation.

The good doctor assured me that my life would be a lot easier if I no longer had to bear this atrocious burden. My family and my friends encouraged me to go ahead with it, reminding me to what point I had suffered before deciding to amputate the right leg.

-Amputation of my left leg at the Montreal General Hospital

So once again I made the decision: December 29, 2009, they amputated my left leg at the Montreal General Hospital. Before going to the operating room I couldn't help but feel that I was going to my own execution: after taking some blood and my vital signs the nurse opened the curtains where my family was waiting to wish me well and said, "Okay, you can say your **good-byes** now!"

I stayed 2 weeks at this hospital. I was eager to get back my autonomy. I learned quickly how to transfer from my bed to the wheelchair and from the wheelchair to the toilet.

-Rehabilitation at the Montreal Rehabilitation Institute
Afterwards - just like the time of my first amputation 4 years earlier, I went to the Montreal Rehabilitation Institute. I stayed there for 3 weeks.

This time the specialists told me that they wouldn't give me a prosthesis because it would be 4 times harder to use than it had been with the first one. Instead, they showed me how to be as independent as possible without my legs.

-You have to say that I was determined!
The fact of no longer having any legs, did it represent a big change in my life? I would say no: I've been using my wheelchair for 27 years: I could do my regular transfers, get into a car... I could still drive the car that my father had had adapted for me.

-Let's look at the bright side of things
There is an interesting side of my new situation: finished are the daily bandaging and the pains of the last 28 years!

Farewell to the horrible pains of my lower limbs!

Farewell to infections, antibiotics, gloves and bandages!

Farewell to the nurses and I never have to worry about ulcers which could develop on my legs!

I could therefore restart my activities
Obviously I can no longer put my wheelchair in the car myself, but I can, thanks to the Adapted Transport Service and friends, take up all my activities again. If I want to get somewhere, there's always a way!

EPILOGUE

MY FATHER

SINCE MY MOTHER'S PASSING, MY FATHER AND I NOW LIVE ALONE AT THE HOUSE

My father is a good and very generous family man: he always worked hard so that we could all live well, my mother and the 4 children.

When I was young, I felt that he really loved me a lot: he used to spoil me, the youngest of the family. Later on, throughout my health problems, his love for me never waned: he never complained about the increase of worries and of work that I imposed upon him.

My father always kept himself busy. He ran a plumbing shop, he actively participated in the B'nai B'rith Organization, the synagogue, made time to attend weekly practices of the Barbershoppe group "The South Shore Saints" and take part in their concerts, etc., etc., etc. He also liked to play cards with his friends. He was the life of the party whom everyone enjoyed because of his personality and singing voice: he didn't wait to be asked to sing and lead others to sing.

My father always represented the authority of the family. When I was young, he used to give me a lot of freedom, but also a lot of advice… very firm! He likes to be in control of the situation.

Since the beginning of my health problems, I know that he feels very badly for everything I've undergone and does everything he can to accommodate me. I can count on his love and his support. He always encourages me to go forward. As I get older, we develop a healthy man-to-man relationship.

Since my mother's death, without speaking about it too often, we share the same pain and this brings the 2 of us a lot closer.

And Me....

To pour out my heart and express my feelings: that's not me.

To say that I am incensed because of everything that happened to me: that's not me.

To say that I am jealous of others who can do anything they please: that's not me.

Obviously I cannot say that I am content with my physical condition: it's a daily struggle which slows me down, but does not prevent me from going forward in life and to derive pleasure from it!

No one ever told me that life was going to be easy. My philosophy is to expect the worst and if anything good happens, it's a bonus! I live my life.

Unfortunately, due to the dose of radiation I received I cannot have any children... but I value my celibacy: I have a big family and lots of friends. There is my support.

I always accepted what I was given and I try to make the best of it. Thank you life!

MY EXPERIENCE TEACHING

1- Teaching youngsters

In 1986, Royal Vale Elementary School, now located in Notre-Dame de Grace, called me to ask if I'd be interested in running a games class as a supplemental activity 3 hours a week.

This program responded to a new objective in education: exposing children to a large range of activities: computers, arts, cooking, theatre, etc...

I taught games like checkers, cards, chess, etc.

Three years later, they narrowed the games down to chess alone, considering all the pedagogical benefits of this game: concentration, discipline, opening the spatio-temporal dimension and respect for your opponent in a competition. They asked me to teach it to students from grades 1 through 6.

I like working with children: they make me laugh by their spontaneity and their innocent reactions. For them, the contact with a teacher in a wheelchair is a new experience. They want to know everything: why I am in a wheelchair, what happened to my legs, if it hurts, if it's difficult for me to get around and if I could go fast! One kid said as he saw me zip down the hall, "There goes Wheelman!". Another one said to me, "But you're hurt. How can you be alive?"

It brings me pleasure to see the smile of these youngsters and, at the same time, to note that they are experiencing without dramatizing it, an aspect of life that was unknown to them up until now.

Currently I am at 4 schools a few hours a week. Three of these schools are situated in the east end of the city, far from where I live. I get there thanks to the Adapted Transport Service – an excellent service of the city of Montreal which brings me from door to door.

2- Private tutoring
In addition to my courses to the youngsters, I receive students and adults at home: nurses, business people and professionals, for private lessons in French, English, Spanish and mathematics.

I find a lot of satisfaction in private tutoring.

Moreover, the fact that these people come to my house makes the job easier. Teaching 1 person at a time makes the lesson more personal, more efficient and more interesting.

I'm always looking for new students.

Bernard Gotlieb surrounded by members of Scrabble® club #83 at Trudeau Park in Cote St. Luc

MY EXPERIENCE AS DIRECTOR OF A SCRABBLE® CLUB

Since the founding of my Scrabble® club in 1978, I have a list of 25 regular players of whom an average of 16 come every week. We have players of all levels: experts who have memorized the dictionary, intermediate players and beginners.

-My role as director
As director, I try to satisfy everyone in pairing up players of the same strength. I take in all the results and distribute weekly prizes for different categories at random: the person with the highest score, the most improved player, etc.

At the end of each month, I organize a mini-club tournament of 4 games. The players like this competition which differs from regular club play. In addition to these tasks, I collect the weekly charge and I coordinate who will take care of the snacks.

My players have always supported me. They have encouraged me too and have been extremely generous to me. Every week for a number of years my friend Fran would pick me up and put my wheelchair in the trunk of her car. Sary, another good friend from the club, has taken over this favour for the past several years. I am indebted to both of them.

Throughout all these years around 200 players have passed through my club. I am very proud of this club that has produced 2 world champions: Joel Wapnick and Dave Boys (I've become friends with him).

The club is now a big "family", happy to see each other every week. And I am happy to think that it is I who started all this.

LETTER FROM DR. ROBIN BILLICK

Head of the Department of Dermatology at the Jewish General Hospital

You came to me as a young patient having survived a new therapy for acute leukemia – a bone marrow transplant. Your leukemia was in remission, however both you and I realized that 1 set of complications replaced another. Life with a chronic debilitatory disease is both a physical and mental drain and perhaps one can only achieve contentment/satisfaction or acceptance if the negative energies are channeled into something productive.

The study of your case helped advance research. In effect an article was published under the title "bacillary angiomatosis (eruptive hemangiomas) in a patient with graft-versus-host disease".

Optimal therapy in a background of GVHD's sclerosis with poor circulation could only result in a below knee amputation – a devastating blow to you who sought to be as active and mobile as possible...

Complication upon complication; cancer upon leukemia therapy, debility physically in a young brilliant person with incredible potential certainly squeezed and compromised your ability to succeed in a normal life.

However, your courage to survive despite the catastrophes in your condition is in itself a testimony: you persist in teaching and have the elasticity of mind to play Scrabble®. This is a commendation to your brilliance and to your human endeavour.

The writing of your history and perspective will potentially enlighten others to the suffering you have endured, and how it has made you a more determined and resilient individual.

Sincerely,
Robin

LETTER FROM DR. HANS A. MESSNER

Chief of the Department of Hematology at the Princess Margaret Hospital in Toronto

Dear Bernie,

As a young man of nineteen, you accepted to embark on a long and arduous process which is still going on today after 30 years. It was all about you continuing to live ... You had to face, in the summer of 1979, a choice between the generally conservative treatments at the time and the yet to be proven strategy of a bone marrow transplant.

With the unwavering support of your family, you chose the latter. Your sister Gloria was completely willing to be the donor; she proudly withstood the pain associated with the collecting of the bone marrow.

And yes, you were right: in 1996, 17 years after the transplant, your name was mentioned in a medical journal talking about the recipients of a bone marrow transplant for leukemia: you are the second longest-surviving bone marrow transplant patient for chronic myelogenous leukemia in the world.

When a big mention is made to successes in medicine, too often the extraordinary individuals, who accept to pay the high price, are forgotten. You are one of them ...

The severe chronic disease which followed, deprived you of your legs. And yet, your spirit overcame and you accept to share your experience and your love of life with us all.

Thank you,

Hans Messner

To all those who allowed me to physically and mentally survive, thank you

In my misfortune of being stricken with leukemia, I was very fortunate to have been followed by excellent doctors. Without their care and their total dedication, I would not be here today. Dear doctors, thank you for life!

Dr. Caplan,
From the moment you diagnosed my leukemia, you thoroughly took care of me. Conscientious and hard-working, you were always there for me no matter how busy you were.

It is you who diagnosed my leukemia, who followed me for the subsequent months and who admitted me to the hospital when I went into blast crisis; it is you who made all the arrangements with the Princess Margaret Hospital in Toronto where I was able to receive a bone marrow transplant.

You also took care of me when I returned from Toronto; it is you again who found the specialists who I needed through the years that followed the transplant.

I infinitely thank you for everything you've done for me.

Dr. Messner,
You, the father of the bone marrow transplant program for Canada, how could I thank you enough for your dedication to me?

During my hospitalization at the Princess Margaret, you examined me daily; you answered all my questions and appeased all my fears; you devoted a lot of time and it is you who took charge of the whole procedure.

Your competence as well as your kindness, your patience, your wisdom and the personal interest you manifested for me have always reassured me. I put my trust in you: you gave me hope and made me feel, with your warm smile, that everything would go well.

I am indebted to you for having saved my life. Thank you for life!

Dr. Billick,
For more than 25 years, you've been my dermatologist. You have always shown yourself to be more than sympathetic towards me. I felt your compassion: it was as if you were suffering with me. You always found time for me despite your unbelievably busy schedule, and you would discuss my case with your medical students.

I want to really thank you for all the interest and care you have shown me. I enormously appreciate your constant efforts in researching new approaches in wound healing.

Lincoln D'Souza, nurse clinician at the Royal Victoria Hospital
You also, Lincoln D'Souza, I thank you very much for your good care and untiring efforts to heal my leg ulcers. You never stopped looking for new ways of relieving my suffering.

Thanks to your humour, you made me relaxed while undoing and changing my bandages and I always left your clinic laughing. Thank you!

Dear nurses,
As well, all of you who have been at my side to give me care and to help me, as much physically as morally – you are my "guardian angels".

My big, dear family,
As for you, each and every member of my warm family, I don't know if I could have overcome my trials without your constant support and love.

How could I thank you for your devotion throughout all these years? I am blessed to have such a close family.

And finally, dear Gloria,
I owe you everything; you gave me your bone marrow. Without you, very dear sister, nothing would have been possible. How could I ever thank you for life?

Thank you from all my heart for this chance to live: you are my hero!

Bernard Gotlieb

APPENDIX

- ADVANCES IN MEDICINE TO TREAT LEUKEMIA IN THE LAST 30 YEARS

- MY PERCEPTION OF THE PROGRESS MADE IN MEDICINE – AS BEING THE FIRST SURVIVOR IN CANADA OF A BONE MARROW TRANSPLANT FOR LEUKEMIA

- THE NATIONAL CANCER INSTITUTE

- THE LEUKEMIA SOCIETY OF CANADA

MY PERCEPTION OF THE PROGRESS IN MEDICINE FOR THE TREATMENT OF CHRONIC MYELOGENOUS LEUKEMIA

The progress made in medicine for treating leukemia over the past 30 years has been, according to me, fantastic!

According to the magazine "Source" (spring, 2009), "with new drugs and new combinations, the future for people living with CML seems to be very promising."

The health condition and age of the CML patient will determine the kind of treatment they'll receive. The most effective treatment is the targeted therapies which target specific genes. Since May, 2001, the American Food and Drug Administration approved the use of Imatinib as a first treatment for people with CML. Gleevec is the most used drug that contains the active ingredient "Imatinib Mesylate" which inhibits the growth of abnormal white cells by killing the leukemic cells in the bone marrow. Gleevec allows the return of the normal blood production of red and white blood cells as well as platelets. It can be taken for life. In the case where it does not yield results, there are second and third generations of Imatinib which could be used (Sprycel and Tasigna).

Among other treatments are chemotherapies, multiple drugs or biological therapies where a patient's immune system is used to block the leukemia: examples are Interferon, monoclonal antibodies, or even a type of protein made in the lab that destroys leukemic cells.

The bone marrow transplant or the stem-cell transplant are not always necessary but are still viable options. These may be used for patients whose disease is more advanced or for those who have tried Gleevec and have not had success. Some people want to do a bone marrow transplant but have no donor (about 20% have no match).

Today, for the 2 types of bone marrow transplants - allogenic (from a donor) and autologous (from oneself), it's rarer to take the bone marrow from the pelvis area (as they did with my sister Gloria under general anesthetic). It's much more common to collect stem cells from the blood at an external clinic (the procedure is called "apheresis", similar to the cell-separator machine). The transplant has been simplified since I had mine and patients don't stay as long in hospital.

Personal remark:
"Since the transplant was experimental back then, I knew I was a guinea pig. However, I am the longest surviving bone marrow transplant patient for leukemia in Canada, second in the world. Considering the advances in modern medicine for the treatment of leukemia, I still think I was born 30 years too early!"

Bernard Gotlieb